CURRENT
PROBLEMS
IN REFERENCE
SERVICE

· ·

by Tho̲ ̲ ̲ ̲ ̲vin

R. R. BOWKER COMPANY
New York & London, 1971

Published by R.R. Bowker Company (A Xerox Company)
1180 Avenue of the Americas, New York, N.Y. 10036

Copyright © 1971 by Xerox Corporation
International Standard Book Number: 0–8352–0425–1
Library of Congress Catalog Card Number: 77–162527
Printed and bound in the United States of America.

If you're thinking about 'light,' 'wall,' 'table'
then they have to be somewhere. A chair in Alaska
is not the same as a chair in Florida. A chair in
Florida is some place to stretch out in. A chair
in Alaska is some place to huddle up in. And a
lamp at noon is not the same thing as a lamp at
midnight. So there's someplace—you need some sort
of a weather to make them all hang together.

"An Interview With Kenneth Koch"
UNIVERSITY REVIEW, February 1970

CONTENTS

• • • • • • • • • • • •

PREFACE

· · · · · · · · · · ·

The publication of this volume marks the inauguration of the new Bowker Series in "Problem-Centered Approaches to Librarianship." The new series is designed to make case studies available for instructional use in all major areas of the library school curriculum, as well as to demonstrate the value of the case study as a vehicle for presentation and analysis of professional problems. Future volumes in the series will appear at regular intervals and will focus on such areas as school media programs, cataloging and classification, the literature of science and technology, the development of academic library book collections, computer applications, and problems of middle-management in libraries. It is my privilege to serve as the Editor of the series.

Current Problems in Reference Service is a collection of thirty-five new problem case studies intended for instructional use in both formal and informal teaching-learning situations in the field of librarianship. Experience with my earlier collection, *Problems in Reference Service* (New York: R.R. Bowker, 1965), has made it clear that case studies such as these can be used not only in classroom situations, but also in the pre-service and in-service training of library personnel. I hope that the choice of case studies included in this volume may also make it applicable to the purposes of workshops, institutes, conferences and similar types of training environments for librarians, without detracting from its usefulness in the library school classroom.

This volume represents an entirely new collection of case studies, rather than a revision of *Problems in Reference Service*. Together with the earlier volume, it brings to sixty-five the total number of published case studies in general reference available under the Bowker imprint. As the title of the present collection implies, the emphasis here is on case studies that deal with issues of current concern to reference librarians and library administrators (such as service to the disadvantaged and to minority groups, reference inquiries in controversial or sensitive areas, application of performance budgeting to reference service, and the like) by contrast with the cases in the earlier volume, many of which reflected classic or perennial problems in the reference field. Thus, this volume can be used by teachers of basic reference, either independently or in conjunction with the earlier collection.

The extent to which I have valued and benefited from the responses and reactions of both teaching colleagues in other institutions and practicing librarians to the kinds of case studies included in *Problems in Reference Service* may be underestimated by those among them who find that, by and large, the same types of problems are represented here in about the same proportions as in the earlier collection. To these good friends, I can report only that those who called for elimination of, or reduction in, the number of "method" case studies in favor of "policy" cases were almost exactly counterbalanced numerically by those who suggested precisely the opposite. Under such circumstances, one is reduced to the seemingly selfish alternative of keeping one's own counsel. I have therefore attempted to strike the kind of balance between method and policy that seems to me most comfortable and appropriate to my own teaching objectives in the introductory reference course, recognizing that probably only a minority of students in this core course will ever actually do reference work in libraries, but that almost all will, directly or indirectly, influence, or be influenced by, the level and quality of reference/information service offered in the libraries with which they are associated.

The order in which the case studies in this volume are arranged also reflects little more than my personal preferences in organizing the content of the introductory reference course. Among the case studies relating chiefly to the location of specific information in reference sources, those involving primarily the use of bibliographies and indexes precede those that are dependent for solution on a knowledge of dictionaries, encyclopedias, handbooks, biographical or geographical sources. Case studies that relate principally to formulation, interpretation or application of reference policy appear at intervals throughout the book. The order of these represents what I conceive to be a progression from simple to complex, although not every reader will necessarily agree with my judgment of relative difficulty or complexity. I see no reason why anyone using the book for instructional or training purposes need feel constrained to assign the cases in the order in which they are presented here.

In addition to its emphasis on emerging issues and problems, the present volume differs from my earlier collection by the inclusion here of examples of case situations in which the analyst is required to adjudicate among the merits of multiple inquiries presented almost simultaneously by multiple inquirers. Such case studies have been developed in an attempt to simulate a kind of situation that arises frequently in library practice, and to compensate in part for one aspect of the artificiality of the classroom environment, which allows a student hours or days to ponder and investigate a problem that would have to be resolved in a matter of minutes on the job.

Because there has been little fundamental change in the basic instructional format of the case method reference course since the publication of *Problems in Reference Service*, it has not seemed necessary to provide here a detailed description of the case technique as it is applied in the classroom. It is, however, suggested that those unfamiliar with either the objectives or the methods of the case approach in the introductory reference course read the "Introduction" to *Problems in Reference Service*. Similarly, those involved as instructors, leaders or participants in courses or training programs where the case method is used may find it helpful to examine the illustrative solutions to case problems prepared by students in the School of Library Science at Simmons College, which are incorporated both in my own earlier collection of case studies and in those by Kenneth R. Shaffer and Kenneth F. Kister. These volumes, along with a selection of other recent books and articles relating to the application of the case approach to library education and in-service training, are listed in the "Selected Bibliography" appended to this book.

One point from the "Introduction" to my earlier collection does bear repetition here. All of the case studies that follow are based on actual library situations, but none can or should be identified with any single or particular prototype. Each case study in this volume is a composite of two or more problem environments. All names, facts, statistics, geographical and personal relationships have been altered so that the cases, as presented, do not in any degree or sense portray any actual person, place, library or situation. All personal names have been selected, at random, from the list of "Places in the U.S. with Populations Exceeding 2,500" which appears in *The World Almanac and Book of Facts.* With one or two obviously fictitious exceptions (e.g., "Metro University"), all names of cities, towns and institutions have been taken from the list of rivers outside the United States which appears in the *Standard Encyclopedia of the World's Rivers and Lakes* (New York: Putnam, 1965).

ACKNOWLEDGMENTS

· ·

In the course of discussing new titles for the Bowker Series in "Problem-Centered Approaches to Librarianship," I have learned much from my fellow authors both about the library specializations represented by their individual contributions and about other styles in case method and problem-oriented instruction. I acknowledge with respect and gratitude the many benefits I have derived from these associations, as well as the invaluable assistance of colleagues both at Simmons College and elsewhere who have been generous in sharing their experiences in case method teaching with me and in helping me to see more clearly the shortcomings of my own earlier work.

Neither this volume nor its predecessor would have been written were it not for the advice and support of Professor Kenneth R. Shaffer, Director of the School of Library Science, Simmons College. He was the first to suggest to me, more than a decade ago, that the case technique could be adapted to the reference area, and to demonstrate to me, through his own work, precisely how this might be done. I am deeply indebted to Professor Shaffer, as well as to my distinguished colleague at the Library School of George Peabody College, Professor Frances Neel Cheney, whose continuing interest in the development and use of case materials in the reference field has been a source of constant encouragement.

I also wish to acknowledge here the invaluable assistance of Patricia Martinson in the preparation of the manuscript for this book, and of Robert Landau, Carole Collins, Madeline Miele and Rona Morrow of the Book Editorial Department of the R.R. Bowker Company, who successively advised me on behalf of the publisher.

Students, former students, alumni and professional friends have been a major source of library experiences and problems that have ultimately found their way into case study form for this book. To all, I take this opportunity to acknowledge collectively contributions too numerous to list individually. But beyond any of these, I thank my family for their infinite patience and unbounded affection.

Current Problems in Reference Service

• •

1.
A Charge of
Discrimination

· · · · · · · · · · ·

Dorothea Lykens, Director of Instructional Resources at Volta Valley State College, sighed wearily as she read for the third time the memorandum which had arrived in the morning's interdepartmental mail:

To: Dr. Lykens
From: Charles Shamokin

The Joint Faculty-Student Committee on Student Life will meet at 2 p.m. on Friday, February 6 to review the charges of discrimination against Mexican-American students which have been made against Mr. Yeadon of the library staff. This matter has been referred to the Committee for investigation by Dr. Slatingon, Vice-President for Administrative Affairs. It is the intention of the Committee to receive relevant testimony from all concerned parties, review the charges and, subsequently, make a recommendation to Dr. Slatington with respect to Mr. Yeadon's continuance as a member of the college staff.

As you know, the charges against Mr. Yeadon have become a matter of public knowledge both on the campus and at the state level, as a consequence of newspaper publicity. The Committee wishes to conduct its inquiry in a manner that will ensure calm and rational examination of the charges, determination of their basis, if any, in fact, and scrupulous objectivity with respect to the interests of all concerned. For this reason, I am particularly appreciative of your willingness, as expressed during our telephone conversation yesterday, to appear before the Committee, and to make available a summary of Mr. Yeadon's employment record with the college.

As I told you on the telephone, Mr. Yeadon has received written notice of this meeting and has been invited to testify with respect to the allegations against him. Beyond this, he has been offered the opportunity to be present during the entire hearing, and to be accompanied by an adviser or counsel of his choice, if he so desires. I believe that he has also been urged to attend the Committee sessions by Dr. Slatington. Regrettably, Mr. Yeadon has indicated that he will neither present his side of the matter to the Committee nor attend the hearings. I hope you may be able to persuade him to alter this decision, because I believe it is clearly in the best interest of all concerned that he be present in order to respond to the accusations made against him.

> Charles Shamokin
> Chairman, Committee on Student Life
> Associate Professor of Biology

Dr. Lykens was appointed Director of Instructional Resources at Volta Valley six years ago. Established before World War II as a teacher-training institution, Volta Valley, which is located near a large metropolitan area, has grown to the size of a small university in recent years. The college now offers undergraduate and graduate degrees in some thirty liberal arts and professional fields and has an enrollment of over 9,000 students. About 300 of the college's 6,000 undergraduates have come to Volta Valley under a special recruiting program for minority groups. Among these are nearly 150 students of Mexican-American and Spanish-American ancestry, drawn from both urban and rural areas within the state where the college is located and by which it is supported. This special recruiting program is in its third year of operation.

Martin Yeadon's employment record shows that he holds a baccalaureate degree in French literature from a distinguished liberal arts college, and that he joined the staff of the Volta Valley State College library twenty-three years ago, immediately after graduation from library school. He was appointed to the staff by Dr. Lykens' predecessor, a former member of the teaching faculty at Volta Valley, who had held the position of library director for nearly twenty years without benefit of formal academic training in librarianship. As Mr. Yeadon has often mentioned to younger members of the staff and to Dr. Lykens, he had the distinction of having been the first professionally trained librarian employed at Volta Valley. Prior to his arrival, there had been no formal reference service available. Such assistance as was available to the then small faculty and student body was provided informally by various members of the library staff manning the circulation desk. During his twenty-three years of service at Volta Valley, a new library building has been constructed, the collections have been increased from 30,000 to over 300,000 volumes, and the staff of the reference department has grown to four professional librarians with supporting clerical staff. In recognition of this last development, Dr. Lykens, shortly after her arrival at Volta Valley, had changed the title of Mr. Yeadon's position to Chief Reference Librarian. As head of the reference department, Mr. Yeadon reports directly to Dr. Lykens. At age fifty-five, it seems clear that Mr. Yeadon has no ambitions beyond his present position, and that he apparently expects to occupy the post of Chief Reference Librarian until he reaches the mandatory retirement age ten years from now.

Dr. Lykens reflected, as she pondered the problem before her, that there would have been no reason, up until two years ago, to doubt that Mr. Yeadon would have been able to do precisely that. Professionally, he was respected both within the library and by the faculty of the college as an able reference librarian and an efficient department head. For some years, in addition to providing instruction to incoming freshmen in the use of the library, each semester Mr. Yeadon has taught a course in bibliography at the graduate level, which has attracted students from a number of departments with the blessing of their academic advisers. As a personality, Dr. Lykens thought of Mr. Yeadon as businesslike, somewhat reserved, but "pleasant." She had the impression, although Mr. Yeadon did not often discuss such matters with his co-workers, that his social life was perhaps a limited one, even for a single man his age. Although as a state employee he was prohibited by law from taking a direct part in political activities, Dr. Lykens was aware from comments Mr. Yeadon had made that he was well-informed about current issues and enthusiastically supported conservative candidates for public office.

The arrival on the Volta Valley campus of the first group of students under the special recruiting program for minority groups had been a new and, in some respects, a difficult experience for almost every member of the college staff. It appeared to be especially difficult for Mr. Yeadon. During the first year of the program, isolated comments and complaints about Mr.

Yeadon's relationships with students in this group had come directly or indirectly to Dr. Lykens, but these had not seemed serious enough to lead
her to take any action. In the second year, however, the problem, which
Dr. Lykens had hoped would correct itself as Mr. Yeadon became more
accustomed to dealing with students from minority groups, became instead
much more acute. Dr. Lykens began to receive reports that Mr. Yeadon
was rude to these students, that he refused them help at the reference desk
or provided only minimal assistance with seeming reluctance, and that he
frequently made sarcastic or disparaging remarks about them in their presence or in the presence of other students and faculty. Dr. Lykens learned
from members of the staff that Mr. Yeadon opposed the policy of the college in attempting to recruit minority group students in large numbers. He
had denounced this as "the ruin of the college," both to other members of
the staff and to library users, and he was particularly outspoken in his con-
demnation of what he considered special concessions to Mexican-American
students. Reports reached Dr. Lykens that Mr. Yeadon had, on more than
one occasion, referred to students in this group by several particularly un-
attractive racial epithets.

Midway through the academic year, Dr. Lykens began to receive complaints directly from individual students in the minority group program
about Mr. Yeadon. Because of these, and because she sensed that the matter had become disturbing to some members of the staff, she somewhat re-
luctantly scheduled a conference with Mr. Yeadon. She began on a positive
note by expressing her admiration for the general quality of his work in the
reference department and her genuine respect for his professional abilities.
Then, speaking quite directly, although as tactfully as possible, she told
Mr. Yeadon that complaints had been made about the quality of reference
service being provided to some members of the student body, particularly
Mexican-American students, and that she wished to bring these complaints
to his attention. Mr. Yeadon's response was immediate and direct. Quite
calmly, and without any trace either of emotion or resentment, he thanked
Dr. Lykens for bringing this matter to his attention and assured her that it
was his personal policy, as well as the policy of the reference department, to
provide "fair and equal service to all students." "Quite frankly, Dr. Lykens,"
Mr. Yeadon continued, "I find it most distressing that complaints of this
kind against me should have reached your ears. I'm sorry if the Chicano
students feel they are somehow being 'discriminated against' in the library.
Sorry and surprised and shocked, because, if anything, I have personally

bent over backwards to help these students and work with them. Believe me, Dr. Lykens, it is not easy to help these students. These youngsters simply don't have any background to prepare them for college. And I really find it disheartening when, instead of taking advantage of the opportunity they've been given here, they go around dreaming up imaginary instances of discrimination as an excuse for their own failures."

As they continued to discuss the complaints, Mr. Yeadon simply repeated his assurances that all students received absolutely equal treatment at the reference desk and that accusations of discrimination on his part against Mexican-American students simply had no basis in fact. In response to a question from Dr. Lykens, he said very frankly that he was personally opposed to the college's minority group recruiting program, because he felt it had led to a "double-standard" in grading and to a general lowering of academic standards. Mr. Yeadon said that in his opinion neither the cause of social justice nor the academic world would benefit from this program, and that, in the long run, the minority group students themselves would come to resent the double standard as a badge of racial inferiority. Nonetheless, he stated unequivocally that since the college had decided to recruit and educate minority group students in this way, he considered these students legitimate members of the college community in every respect and fully entitled to every service which the library made available to students on "an absolutely equal basis."

As she reflected on this initial conference, Dr. Lykens recalled that she had admired Mr. Yeadon's maturity and forthrightness in discussing the complaints against him. She recognized that his reservations about the recruitment of minority group students were probably shared by a significant number of faculty and staff. She accepted his assurances that all students were afforded equal treatment at the reference desk, and hoped that by bringing the complaints to his attention he would guard against any inadvertent act or statement which might be construed as a racial slur. The complaints against Mr. Yeadon from Mexican-American students had continued, however, and had become even more frequent and intense in the current year. Two student groups had filed written complaints with Dr. Lykens. In addition to repeating the charges of discrimination at the reference desk, these groups also accused Mr. Yeadon of discrimination in hiring student assistants and in grading student papers, which were part of the compulsory freshman library orientation and affected grades in the freshman English course. Several emotional letters to the student newspaper stimulated an editorial crusade calling for Mr. Yeadon's dismissal, and this in turn was picked up as a news item in newspapers all over the state. Shortly after midyear examinations, the Mexican-American student group had formally demanded of the college administration that Mr. Yeadon be dismissed from the staff, and the administration had referred the matter to the Faculty-Student Committee on Student Life for investigation, as indicated in Professor Shamokin's memorandum to Dr. Lykens.

These developments had, needless to say, occasioned several further conferences between Dr. Lykens and Mr. Yeadon. In each of these discussions, Mr. Yeadon had maintained that the charges of discrimination against him were totally unjustified. He admitted that the amount of time and assistance which he gave to individual students varied, but he maintained that this was a matter of judgment on his part based on the complexity of the inquiry, the extent of the individual student's need for assistance, and the demands on his time at any given moment. He said that the problem exercises used in the freshman library orientation were objective multiple-choice tests, and allowed for little or no subjectivity in grading. He readily admitted that no Mexican-American students were currently employed in the reference department, but indicated that none had applied for employment in his department during the current year. Mr. Yeadon suggested that incoming Mexican-American students were "indoctrinated" by their predecessors to the notion that he was a "racist" and that there was simply nothing he could do to alter his image with that segment of the student community.

In her conversations with administrative officers of the college about Mr. Yeadon, Dr. Lykens had indicated that whatever his limitations might be in dealing with Mexican-American students, these must be weighed against his years of devoted and capable service to the college and his success in carrying out all of the other responsibilities of the position of Chief Reference Librarian. She stated that she had never personally witnessed any instance of rudeness or discrimination on his part toward any individual student, and that no member of the library staff had ever complained to her about Mr. Yeadon's treatment of students. She said that she felt some of the complaints that had been registered against Mr. Yeadon by individual students were petty and trivial, and that in her opinion he might, to some extent, be the victim of circumstances. While admitting that Mr. Yeadon's image with minority group students was not as favorable as it might be, Dr. Lykens had, up to now, taken the position that there were no adequate grounds for dismissing him or transferring him to another job in the library.

The latter would, in her view, have been an impracticable course of action in any event, since there was no other department headship open for which Mr. Yeadon would be qualified by interest or experience.

After considering the Shamokin memorandum for more than an hour, Dr. Lykens telephoned Mr. Yeadon and asked him to come to her office for a short conference. When questioned, he said that he had indeed refused to attend or take part in the upcoming hearings of the Committee on Student Life. Mr. Yeadon said that he felt he should not be required to defend himself against accusations which he described as "both unjust and totally unwarranted" before a committee which had no jurisdiction over him as a member of the library staff. "Dr. Lykens," he concluded, *"you* are my supervisor. If you believe that I have been lying to you, if you have evidence to support the charges that have been made against me, or if you consider any personal shortcomings that I may have in dealing with these students sufficient grounds for dismissal, then *you* should recommend to the administration that my contract not be renewed. If you do not intend to dismiss me, then I think I have the right to expect you to defend my interests before this Committee and the administration. I know you are planning to speak to the Committee on Friday, and I understand several members of the department and the library staff have also asked to speak on my behalf. I realize that my decision not to appear before the Committee may make it more difficult for you in this respect, and may result in my being judged guilty *in absentia.* But my principles simply will not allow me to give in to this kind of harassment and be the willing victim of a kangaroo court. I'm sorry, but that is my final decision."

• • • • •

If you were Dr. Lykens, how would you respond to Mr. Yeadon's final statement? Would you accept his refusal to appear before the Committee on Student Life?

Do you believe that Mr. Yeadon's attitude toward Mexican-American students as revealed in this case warrants his dismissal from the post of Chief Reference Librarian? Or do you feel that Dr. Lykens has been correct in resisting student and administrative pressures to transfer or dismiss him? Can a person like Mr. Yeadon, who has become so unpopular with a segment of the student community, be allowed to continue in a post as sensitive as that of Chief Reference Librarian?

2.
A Request
from a Teacher
· · · · · · · · · · ·

Among the items of morning mail delivered to the desk of Carol Vinton, Chief of the Reference Division of the Q___ State Library, was the following letter addressed to the state librarian:

Dear Sir:

I wonder if you will help me locate a book for which I have been searching? It is a children's book called "Tell Me A Story." We used to borrow it regularly from the library in our northern California town when I was a little girl (in the 1940's). There are wonderful stories in it, with a long and a short version of each, which I remember after all these years. One, for example, told of the adventures of a family who had to take all the farm animals into the house because their barn became flooded.

I am now teaching a course for preschool teachers and would love to include some of these stories in my class sessions on storytelling. By this time, of course, the book has long been out of print and long gone from the library shelves.

If you could let me know where I might find a copy of this book to buy (no matter how battered and bruised, as long as it is still readable), or arrange for me to borrow a copy long enough to refresh my acquaintance with the stories, it would not only make me happy, but also provide enjoyment for many nursery school children of my students.

I don't know if the state library would carry this book or not, but neither the public library nor the one bookstore in our little town has been able to help me find it, so I am writing to you.

Sincerely yours,

Elizabeth Acton

Miss Vinton noted that the letter bore the return address of a small town within the state and carried a handwritten note from the state librarian asking that the letter be answered by the reference division on his behalf.

The Q____ State Library is one of the strongest and best supported state library agencies in the country at the present time. It is organized administratively into two major units, a legislative reference bureau and a general library services bureau, both housed in the state capitol building. The reference division of the general library services bureau, of which Miss Vinton is in charge, maintains an extensive general reference collection comprising nearly 5,000 volumes, including all the major American and British national, trade, and special subject bibliographies, serial indexes, and the like. The reference division is also responsible for a collection of nearly 200,000 monographs, as well as current and back files of some 300 periodicals and newspapers, all selected to supplement the collections in local public libraries around the state. A union catalog, reflecting chiefly the acquisitions over the last five years of approximately fifty public libraries of varying sizes within the state which subscribe to a cataloging service offered by the state library, and a union list showing the serial holdings of most of the major public and academic libraries in the state are also available in the reference division.

After reading Miss Acton's letter, Miss Vinton first consulted the union catalog, but was not greatly surprised to find that the title did not appear as an entry there, since the union catalog was largely confined to books published in the last five or six years. Moreover, she knew that most of the participating libraries did not purchase cards for juvenile titles from the state. She also consulted the catalog of the state library's own collection, but did not find the book listed there either.

• • • • •

Assuming you were in Miss Vinton's place, and had available to you the reference collection of the Q____ State Library, how would you go about locating the book sought by Miss Acton? Is it possible to find a copy that might be made available to her through interlibrary loan? If a library copy can be located, precisely what would be the procedure for arranging an interlibrary loan, and what would be the appropriate role of the state library, if any, in making these arrangements on Miss Acton's behalf? Are there book dealers who specialize in books of this kind? How would you reply to Miss Acton's letter?

3.
A Biography of Daniel Webster

· · · · · · · · · · · · · ·

"Mrs. Crossett, I need some advice if you have a minute to spare." The speaker was George Tracy, associate professor of American literature, and his remark was directed to Jane Crossett, reference librarian on the staff of the Kolyma College Library. Mrs. Crossett had just returned to the reference desk after her lunch hour to find Dr. Tracy waiting for her. Her conversation with him continued as follows:

MRS. CROSSETT: "Of course. Why don't we sit down here where we can talk? It's nice to see you again. How was your summer?"

DR. TRACY: "Oh, fine, just fine! Lots of sailing and lying around on the beach, but not much work I'm afraid. How about yourself? Busy, I suppose."

MRS. CROSSETT: "We did get away for most of August for a little trip. But, to tell you the truth, at this point, after a week of freshman orientation and library tours, I'm ready for another vacation. Which reminds me, we have another group of them coming in for a tour in about fifteen minutes."

DR. TRACY: "I won't keep you but a minute or two; I just wanted to pick your brain in the hope that you might be able to save me some time. My problem is this. Late last spring, in a moment of folly, I agreed to do a book review for the ____ Journal, which, as you know, is one of the big ones in my field. At the time they wrote me, the book in question hadn't even been published, and I assumed they wanted just a short critical notice. I agreed to do it, and I suppose I shouldn't have because I've got a number of other obligations right now. To make a long story short, the book has appeared about three months earlier than anyone expected, and it seems likely that it will create a bit of a stir, at least in my own rather small circle. So, the editor of the journal would like me to do a full-length review of about 2,500 words or so. The book is a kind of study of Daniel Webster, and I had thought of beginning the review with a résumé of Webster biographies. What I would like to find out is this—when was the *first* biography of Webster published, and who was the biographer? I'm no Webster specialist, but I do know that there was a biography by Knapp that must be one of the first. I don't know the exact date of it, and I don't know if there is anything earlier. I've tried the card catalog here, of course, but we have very little on Webster, and nothing earlier than about 1875. Now, the point is this: I'm facing a deadline and I just don't have time to do any extensive searching. I certainly wouldn't want to burden anyone in the library at such a busy time of year. What I wanted to ask you is whether you would know of any quick way for me to get the name of the author and the date of publication of the first biography of Webster?"

MRS. CROSSETT: "What if there isn't any very quick or simple way to find that out?"

DR. TRACY: "Then I think that it might be better for me to simply omit it from the review."

The Kolyma College Library has a book collection of about 150,000 volumes selected primarily to support instruction at the undergraduate level. The emphasis in the reference collection is on current fact-finding titles rather than bibliographic sources designed for retrospective literature searching. For example, while complete sets of both the *Reader's Guide to Periodical Literature* and the *Social Sciences and Humanities Index* are found on the reference shelves, the library does not own Poole's *Index.* Similarly, the only American period bibliographies available are the *United States Catalog* (1928) and the *Cumulative Book Index.* There is also a set of the printed catalogs of the Library of Congress, excluding *Books: Subjects,* in the cataloging department.

• • • • •

Given the reference sources that are known to be available or might reasonably be expected to be available in the Kolyma College Library, what advice would you give Dr. Tracy if you were Mrs. Crossett?

Who was the author of the earliest biography of Daniel Webster and in what year was it published?

4.
Mutilation of
Reference Books
· · · · · · · · · · · ·

As Roberta Visalia, director of the Fitzroy Public Library, hurried toward the reference room from her office, she tried to decide what course of action to take with respect to the teen-aged boy whom, she had just been informed, was being detained there by the library janitor awaiting her arrival. The boy was well known to the staff as an almost daily visitor to the library. When the reference librarian had called Miss Visalia a few moments earlier to report that Herman Newhall had just been observed by two members of the staff in the act of mutilating the library's newest multi-volume encyclopedia with a razor blade, the library director had recognized his name instantly, because he had been pointed out to her on several previous occasions by various members of the staff as something of a problem.

Herman Newhall was a fourteen-year-old boy who was singularly un-attractive in appearance and manner. His behavior during his frequent visits to the library was variously described by members of the staff as "peculiar," "queer," or "creepy." Several women who were assigned to public service desks had complained often of his alleged blatant voyeurism, and had asked the library janitor to discretely keep an eye on him whenever he was in the building, especially during evening hours.

Herman regularly occupied a seat in the reading room which commanded a clear view of the circulation and reference desks, where, according to the staff, he would remain for hours with a book propped open in front of him, staring at whichever female members of the staff happened to be on desk duty at the time. He suffered from a nervous affliction which caused his head and neck to twitch periodically, as well as from severe

acne. He seemed to be a loner, utterly friendless, and had never been observed to converse with anyone except himself. Periodically, during his
almost daily visits to the library, he would retreat briefly to an isolated
corner of the stack area which could not be observed by the staff, where it
was rumored that he masturbated.

Needless to say, Herman Newhall had, in recent months, been the
subject of frequent conversations in the staff lounge. Through these, Miss
Visalia had learned that, although he was of junior high school age, Herman
had twice failed to be promoted in school and was still in the sixth grade,
that he was considered both intellectually and socially retarded by the Fitzroy school authorities, and that he was generally thought to be emotionally
disturbed by a considerable segment of the juvenile and adult population
of the small suburban community in which the library was located. One of
his teachers had told the children's librarian that all efforts on the part of
school authorities to enlist the support of the boy's parents in dealing with
his obvious problems of personal and social adjustment had met with complete failure. Although neither Miss Visalia nor any other member of the
library staff had ever had any direct contact with the senior Newhalls,
they were reputed to be seriously maladjusted individuals from whom little
or nothing could be expected in terms of constructive efforts to induce a
more normal behavior pattern in their son.

During the past month, both Miss Visalia and the members of her staff
have become concerned at discovering a pattern of seemingly systematic
mutilation of the book collection. This has taken the form of cutting such
words as "communism," "fascism," "national socialist," and the like out
of the pages where they appeared in print (the damage evidently being done
with scissors, knife or razor blade), leaving gaping rectangular holes in the
affected pages. The names "Adolph Hitler," "Benito Mussolini," "Joseph
Stalin," and "Lee Harvey Oswald," along with portraits of these individuals, have been removed from a number of books in similar fashion. The
problem was first detected in the general book collection, where more than
fifty damaged volumes have been identified through a systematic check of
likely classification numbers, and has more recently been found in the reference collection, where a dozen encyclopedia volumes and biographical
dictionaries have been found similarly mutilated. It is estimated that the
replacement costs of the books already known to have been mutilated in
this way would run close to $5,000, including replacement of entire multi-
volume reference sets, where individual volumes cannot be purchased sepa-

rately from the publishers. Since it has not been possible to subject either the entire three hundred volume reference collection or the entire 35,000 volume book collection to a page-by-page inspection, additional damaged volumes may exist that have not yet been identified. Until the apprehension of Herman Newhall in the act of mutilating an encyclopedia, it had been impossible for the staff to determine with certainty whether the damage was being done by a current library user, or whether it had been done at some time in the past, but simply not discovered. Since the problem has only recently come to light, Miss Visalia has not yet had an opportunity to report it to the library board of trustees.

When Miss Visalia arrived at the reference room, she found that Herman Newhall, looking at once frightened, defensive and very hostile, was being detained at one of the reading tables by the library custodian. The assistant in the reference room reported that she and one of the pages had observed the boy in the act of mutilating the pages of an encyclopedia. On the table before Herman lay a damaged volume of the encyclopedia, a razor blade, and several bits of paper which appeared to have been cut from the printed page. When questioned by the reference assistant and the custodian, Herman Newhall denied being responsible for the damage to the book or for having damaged any of the other mutilated volumes with which he had been confronted. The custodian urged Miss Visalia to telephone the town police immediately, requesting that they come to the library and take the boy into custody. The reference assistant concurred in this recommendation, reminding Miss Visalia that destruction of library property was prohibited both by state law and by local ordinance in Fitzroy.

● ● ● ● ●

If you were in Miss Visalia's place, what action would you take with respect to Herman Newhall at this time? Would you turn the boy over to the local police, contact his parents, or attempt to deal with the matter in some other way? What aspects of the total problem situation would have the greatest influence on your decision? What consequences might be anticipated from each of the major courses of action that would be open to Miss Visalia? How would you comment on the manner in which the problem of Herman Newhall as a library user has been handled up to this point?

5.
A Matter
of Public Safety

· · · · · · · · · · · ·

When Joann Dexter, chief of the reference department at Brenta State University Library, arrived at the office of the Director of Libraries, she found the Director, Ralph Muncie, seated at a conference table with three other men whom she did not immediately recognize. As Dr. Muncie introduced her to his guests, however, she remembered having met the first of them, Dr. Winfield, the Vice-President for Administration, on one previous occasion. The other visitors were introduced as George Decatur, newly appointed head of University Security, and Lt. Roger Hawarden of the Subversive Activities Branch of the State Police. After the introductions had been completed, Dr. Winfield opened the discussion:

"Miss Dexter, we're very grateful to you for being willing to join our meeting this morning. I hope that what we say to one another here can remain confidential, because it concerns matters of the greatest sensitivity. Dr. Muncie has assured us that you are a discrete person.

"Now, Miss Dexter, as I'm sure you know, we're going through very difficult times in the history of Brenta. The last academic year was, to say the least, difficult and unpleasant for almost every member of the Brenta community. I'm not sure you are aware of all the incidents that occurred, but I'm certain you must have seen the results of the demonstrations at the Placement Office and the ROTC building. Personally, I feel that our having had to bring National Guard troops onto the campus last May after the administration building was firebombed was the most terrible thing that could have happened to the university. President Bourne and I are determined that such a catastrophe must never occur again at Brenta. We're convinced that we must take steps to restore a climate here where teaching and learning can take place in an atmosphere of calm, rational, objective scholarship. In short, we must stamp out violence on this campus, or the university will be destroyed. You don't want to see this university destroyed, do you, Miss Dexter?"

Miss Dexter indicated that she would not wish to see Brenta State University destroyed. Dr. Winfield continued:

"Neither do I. That is why we are taking preventive steps now, before the opening of the new academic year. As a first step, we have appointed Mr. Decatur, a man of great experience in security matters, to head our campus police, and we have promised him additional manpower this fall to head off trouble before it can develop into a crisis. George, why don't you take over at this point, and explain to Miss Dexter how the library can help you. I know she and Dr. Muncie will want to help the university in every possible way."

Mr. Decatur took the floor at this point, addressing his remarks most directly to Miss Dexter:

"In my experience, the way to deal with trouble is to prevent it. Once somebody throws a rock or fires a weapon or ignites a bomb it's too late, and innocent people get hurt. The answer to this kind of violence is not more violence, but prevention.

"As you know better than I, there were a number of unfortunate incidents on this campus last spring. I don't mean to frighten you, and I certainly would not want what I'm going to say to go beyond this room, but from information which Lt. Hawarden has brought to our attention, we have very good reason to believe that, unless we do something now, there is going to be more serious violence on the campus next fall, and many more people, innocent people, are going to get hurt. We have been informed that Brenta has been selected as a target for the coming year by the radical groups, the groups dedicated to the use of violent means to get their message across. I'm not just talking about relatively harmless forms of student activism like rallies and demonstrations and picketing. I'm talking about a small group of hardcore, violent revolutionaries, some of them adults having no connection with Brenta whatsoever, who take over classrooms and beat up faculty members, who incite minority group students to bring weapons into the dormitories, and who teach kids how to make and use bombs. I'm talking about a group of bums who are a menace to the safety of 12,000 or more people on this campus.

"I gather from the expression on your face that you think Lt. Hawarden and I are exaggerating, but let me assure you that what we're talking about is not just kid stuff. This is serious, dangerous business. Let me just read you a few samples of what this particular group of people we're most concerned about is saying:

> We are very much alive. Last year we attacked the bourgeoisie on the Brenta campus. This year we must build far more militant struggles, turning Brenta into a battleground against the rulers.

> We must show what we stand for and demolish the professor. Try to make classroom insurgency a mass issue right away among the student body at Brenta.

> The days of the pigs are numbered. Last year the thin blue line got worn thinner and thinner. Let's make this year surpass last year! The oppressors must be allowed no peace by day or night, they must be harrassed until their doom.

> To be an assailant or terrorist today is a quality that enobles any honorable man because it is an act worthy of a revolutionary engaged in armed struggle against the military dictatorship and its puppet monstrosities, the universities.

"These are the things that the very people who will be descending on this town and this campus in a few weeks are writing and saying. Believe me, Miss Dexter, Lt. Hawarden and I are not making this up. I wish we were! Unless we can head this off, we are in for serious trouble at Brenta this fall."

Miss Dexter answered, "I certainly dislike the prospect of violence here on the campus as much as anyone, but I don't quite see what the library can do."

"Miss Dexter," Mr. Decatur answered, "that's just what I'm coming to. You are in a position where you have a great deal of contact with students. You also keep records of the use of certain books which are not on the open shelves. I want to ask your help in cooperating with us to identify potential troublemakers so we can head off the trouble through Campus Security before it begins."

"I'm afraid I still don't see what you're after." At this point. Lt. Hawarden spoke for the first time:

"To be specific, Miss Dexter, what Mr. Decatur is asking you to do is note and report to him anything of a suspicious nature that you might observe, so he can check it out. For example, before you came in we were showing Dr. Muncie a handbill that's being distributed to incoming students listing major defense contractors and telling students to demonstrate when they come to recruit on campus. This handbill was compiled right in this library, and before you came down, Dr. Muncie told us you'd mentioned to him that a student or somebody purporting to be a student was in here a couple of weeks ago looking up that very information."

"Yes, that's true, I did mention it to Dr. Muncie. And the boy *was* a student, I know that."

"Can you tell us his name?"

"I'm sorry, I don't know."

"Don't you ask for any identification from people who use the library?"

"Yes, if they want to borrow books. But not at the reference desk."

"Miss Dexter, you were asking a minute ago how the library could help in maintaining order on the campus this coming year. Could I suggest that one thing you could do that would be helpful is to require student identification at the information desk, just as you do when someone wants to borrow a book. In that way, we could know the names of students who might be using the library for purposes that may be destructive to Brenta. I'd like to ask Dr. Muncie if it wouldn't be feasible to institute that kind of system for identification?"

Dr. Muncie said he could see no reason why students could not be required to show identification cards at the reference desk. He made it clear that he deplored the violence that had disrupted the campus in the past year and felt the library should provide every reasonable form of help to the university security force in maintaining order in the future. Miss Dexter next asked Mr. Decatur whether all the members of her staff assigned to the reference desk were being asked to cooperate with the security office. Mr. Decatur said that he would not want Miss Dexter to communicate this to other members of the staff, since he would not want it to become generally known that the library was assisting the security office in this way. Dr. Muncie pointed out that Miss Dexter was in the reference room during most of her working day, and that, simply as a matter of course, she was aware of most of the requests for assistance from students which came across the reference desk, either through observation or through casual conversations with other members of the reference staff.

At this point, Miss Dexter realized that all four men were awaiting a response from her. When she did not reply immediately, Vice-President Winfield said, "Miss Dexter, you look as though you are troubled by what Mr. Decatur and I have asked you to do. I think I can understand that. I'm sure it sounds to you as if you are being asked to 'inform' against students, and nobody relishes playing the role of informer. Also, you may be concerned that some student with a perfectly innocent and legitimate question will be unjustly accused. Nobody, least of all Mr. Decatur or I, intends to let that happen. But our first responsibility is to protect the safety of the vast majority of our students and faculty and people like yourself who are members of the university staff, people who are trying to go about the business of giving or getting an education here. The best way we know to do that is to take steps in advance to prevent any sort of unpleasant or violent incident from occurring. For that purpose, we must have information. Without it, Mr. Decatur and Lt. Hawarden are simply hamstrung. We want them to be able to act before people are hurt or university property is destroyed, as happened last spring, or before some innocent bystander is killed. I think you might find it difficult to live with your conscience if there were a tragedy which you, in any way, might have helped to prevent. I hope that we will not need to ask you for this kind of cooperation indefinitely, but surely you realize that these are not ordinary times. A few people have declared war on this university, and in times like this, the loyalty of every member of the staff to the university is put to the test. The youngsters today have a saying: 'if you're not part of the solution, you're part of the problem.' I think it is just as simple and clearcut as that. We're asking you to become part of the solution to the problem of preventing a small group who care nothing about Brenta University from trying to destroy it."

· · · · ·

If you were in Miss Dexter's place, how would you respond to Mr. Decatur's request for assistance and on what basis would you justify your decision? Is there, as Vice-President Winfield's remarks suggest, a possible conflict here between loyalty to Brenta University on the one hand, and personal or professional ethics on the other? If so, how should the conflict be resolved in this particular situation?

6.
Bibliographic
Assistance
to a Publisher

· · · · · · · · · · ·

The Boyne Memorial Library serves a city of 350,000 in the industrial northeastern United States through a central library and an extensive branch system. Formerly a major center of textile and leather manufacturing, the city of Boyne has, in recent years, undergone a major shift in its economy, as many large mills and plants have moved operations to other areas of the country where labor, materials and transportation are less costly. The city has had to undertake an extensive national program to attract new industries.

The Boyne Industrial Development Commission frequently mentions the library as one of the major assets of the region for new industries. The library is widely recognized as one of the finest in the nation among larger communities. For many years it has flourished under capable leadership and has enjoyed generous financial support from the city. In particular, the Boyne Memorial Library is noted for its strong business reference service. Carol Conroe is the recently appointed head of the library's business department. Miss Conroe came to Boyne two months ago, after ten years of progressively more varied and responsible experience in the business and technology division of one of the largest public libraries in the country.

One afternoon, as she was at work at her desk in the business department office, Miss Conroe received a telephone call from Harmon Brentwood, who began by identifying himself as senior editor of the Havel Press. Their conversation continued as follows:

MR. BRENTWOOD: "Miss Conroe, I've been given your name by one of the people in our accounting department who tells me you were very helpful in finding some information for him a couple of weeks ago. Now, I'm calling because we don't have a library or a librarian here at the Press, and I have a problem that seems to require a librarian's advice. But first, let me ask if you are familiar with Havel?"

MISS CONROE: "Beyond the fact that yours is one of our local companies here in Boyne, I have to be honest, Mr. Brentwood, and say that I know very little about Havel Press. I do have the impression that you are chiefly a publisher of religious books, is that right?"

MR. BRENTWOOD: "Correct on both counts, Miss Conroe. We are located here in Boyne—that is, our trade division has had its editorial offices here since last year. And we have been best known for our religious book publishing activities in the past, although that is changing rather rapidly now. And that's part of the reason for my call. We are trying to expand our list and to develop projects in other areas. As we get into these areas, we're finding that our people don't know enough to cope with some of the problems that arise. Since we're much too small a firm to even think about hiring a librarian, we have to depend on you people to help us out."

MISS CONROE: "Gladly, if we can."

MR. BRENTWOOD: "Tell me, does the library have an art department?"

MISS CONROE: "No, we don't."

MR. BRENTWOOD: "What I am after is a list of all of the artists' sketchbooks that have been published."

MISS CONROE: "That's quite a problem. Before I try to reply, could you be a little more specific about what you want and what you want it for? That might help me to respond more intelligently."

MR. BRENTWOOD: "Well, as I told you, we are looking at a number of possible projects in areas of publishing that would be new to us. One idea we've been considering is a series of paperback reprints of artists' sketchbooks."

MISS CONROE: "I think I understand. You would want to find out which publishers have artists' sketchbooks in print, so you could buy the reprint rights from them."

MR. BRENTWOOD: "Well, actually, we'd probably be more interested in those that are out of print."

MISS CONROE: "Because if the book was out of print, the publisher might be more receptive to selling the reprint rights?"

MR. BRENTWOOD: "Precisely. So, to begin with, we need that complete listing. Is there a list in the library that we could borrow?"

MISS CONROE: "I doubt it, Mr. Brentwood, though I'd have to check the collection to be certain. But let me ask you first—when you say 'all' the sketchbooks that have ever been published, do you really mean *all?*"

MR. BRENTWOOD: "I don't quite follow you on that."

MISS CONROE: "What I'm trying to establish is how comprehensive a list you need. Do you mean all the sketchbooks that have been published since Gutenberg? In all countries of the world? In all languages? By all kinds of publishers, or just by commercial publishers? I mean, do you want a list that would include all the sketchbooks that might have been published by private presses? By museums? Or just commercial publishers?"

MR. BRENTWOOD: "Would that be harder to get?"

MISS CONROE: "At this point, I don't know. It strikes me that what would answer your question is an exhaustive bibliography of published artists' sketchbooks. Whether we have such a bibliography, whether such a bibliography even exists, is something I'll have to check on and call you back. But if I have a more precise idea of just how comprehensive a listing you want, I'll know better whether any bibliography I can locate here will meet the need. Do you see?"

MR. BRENTWOOD: "Yes, I do see. Of course. Well, I guess we'd like the most comprehensive list we could get. Let's see, I don't imagine there'd be the need to go back to Gutenberg."

MISS CONROE: "Just twentieth century publications?"

MR. BRENTWOOD: "I think that's too narrow. We've had some luck with getting reprint rights to nineteenth century books from American publishers."

MISS CONROE: "That's my other question. Is it just American publications you're interested in? Or do you want just English language publications?"

MR. BRENTWOOD: "Well, of course, the language wouldn't make a lot of difference, since it's the illustrations we're interested in."

MISS CONROE: "But surely you don't want—oh, for example—oriental publications, do you? My experience has been that even the so-called comprehensive or exhaustive bibliographies usually only list items in English and in the western European languages."

MR. BRENTWOOD: "Yes, I guess we could say English, American and European publications. That ought to satisfy us, if we can get it."

MISS CONROE: "O.K., that helps to give me enough to go on. Oh, one thing. How much of a rush is there on this?"

MR. BRENTWOOD: "No great hurry. If we could get the list within a month or so, that would be fine."

MISS CONROE: "I think the first thing is to find out for you whether somebody has been kind enough to do a bibliography that will meet your need. If there is one, and we don't own it, we'll try to get a copy for you on interlibrary loan, or tell you where you can buy one, if it's in print."

MR. BRENTWOOD: "Well, I hope there's a bibliography, as you say. Now, what if there isn't? Could we ask you to make one up for us?"

MISS CONROE: "Let's hope there is a bibliography in existence that will give you the information you need. If there isn't, compiling one would be quite a job. I'm afraid compiling extensive bibliographies for individuals or individual companies is something we just can't do here. Especially anything as comprehensive as you seem to want. That would be a very time-consuming job."

MR. BRENTWOOD: "If there isn't a list that you can find for us, what would you suggest we do?"

MISS CONROE: "I guess there really are only two other possibilities. Either drop the project, or have someone compile a bibliography for you."

MR. BRENTWOOD: "How would I go about having a list made? Who would do it?"

MISS CONROE: "Well, librarians are pretty good at that sort of thing. We're trained as bibliographers, you know."

MR. BRENTWOOD (laughing): "I guess I should have figured that out. Tell me, if you can't find a published list of sketchbooks for me, would you or somebody on the staff be able to put a list together for us—sort of, on the side?"

MISS CONROE: "I think members of the staff here do some freelance work from time to time. And I know that the library has no rule against it."

MR. BRENTWOOD: "Perhaps I should ask how much you estimate the cost would be for the kind of list we need?"

MISS CONROE: "You certainly should ask, before you commit yourself or Havel Press to anything that could turn out to be pretty expensive."

MR. BRENTWOOD: "Can you give me a rough idea of the costs?"

MISS CONROE: "Look, Mr. Brentwood, first, let's find out if there is a bibliography in print somewhere that will do the trick for you. If there isn't, then we can discuss compiling one as a freelance project here. I'm just not sure offhand how one would go about it. One problem is that what you're interested in is a form of publication, and most general bibliographies don't index books under form. Offhand, what I'd guess we'd have to do is agree on a list of artists by name—you know, take some standard list of famous artists, and then check the general bibliographies under their names to see if their individual sketchbooks had been published. The other thing that I might mention now is that in compiling comprehensive bibliographies, there is what you might call a 'trade-off' factor at work."

MR. BRENTWOOD: "I don't quite understand what you mean by 'trade-off.' "

MISS CONROE: "Well, you see, first of all, you can't compile a bibliography like this by just consulting one general source. You have to consult a number of bibliographies. If you do this, checking under the names of individual artists, you can fairly easily turn up probably fifty percent of what's been published by just checking a few sources. But, to get the remaining fifty percent, you'd have to check hundreds of additional sources, and that would be both costly and time-consuming in proportion to the number of items that it would produce for the list. Do you see what I mean?"

MR. BRENTWOOD: "I'm not really sure I do."

MISS CONROE: "Well, it doesn't really matter, at this point. Let me check and see if there isn't some neat little bibliography in print somewhere that will answer your need. If there isn't, I'll be glad to give you some suggestions as to how I or someone else here might compile one for you, if you want it, and what I think would be a reasonable cost estimate for compiling bibliographies of varying degrees of comprehensiveness."

Mr. Brentwood agreed readily to this suggestion, and Miss Conroe promised to telephone him within a week. Within a day or two she had checked the library's card catalog, *Bibliographic Index, Besterman,* the *Guide to Art Reference Books,* and the Library of Congress *Books: Subjects* and found no appropriate published bibliography of artists' sketchbooks that appeared to meet the needs of Havel Press.

• • • • •

Assuming that the Boyne Public Library has all of the general and specialized reference sources that one would expect to find in a large, well-stocked public library, what additional steps should Miss Conroe take to determine whether or not a comprehensive bibliography of published artists' sketchbooks exists? Can such a bibliography be located, or would one have to be compiled to meet the needs of Havel Press?

If the compilation of a bibliography is to be undertaken on behalf of Havel Press, what recommendations would you make to Mr. Brentwood concerning its scope, coverage and method of compilation? What estimate of cost would you provide him?

How would you evaluate Miss Conroe's manner of conducting the reference interview, her comments on "trade-off" and form entries, and her subsequent efforts to locate a published bibliography for Mr. Brentwood?

7.
A Bibliography
of D. H. Lawrence
Part I

. . . . . .

Interdepartmental Memorandum
Garonne University
Department of English

From: R. A. Slater, Chairman
To: J. C. Ferguson, Director of Libraries
Re: D. H. Lawrence Checklist

You will, no doubt, recall our recent discussion of a series of bibliographic projects to be carried out by members of your staff and mine, under the general direction of the Department of English. Your response to my inquiry about the feasibility of such projects was sufficient so that I have gone ahead with plans for the first. I am sure you will be pleased to learn that financial support for an annual, annotated D. H. Lawrence Checklist has now been assured, through the generosity of a donor who prefers to remain anonymous. The donor has made available a sum of money that should be adequate to provide for the cost of the first five years of research, publication and distribution of the Checklist to subscribers.

I have agreed to serve as general editor of the Checklist, although I hope in future years to be able to turn this responsibility over to one of the younger men in the department. As you will recall, the plan is to issue the Checklist in March, and to limit each annual issue to books, articles, pamphlets, dissertations, etc. published during the preceding year. Our aim will be to make the list as comprehensive as possible.

If my memory serves me correctly, you agreed that the library might provide weekly lists of new editions of Lawrence's work, and works about him. The English department will take responsibility for annotating the more important titles and editing for publication copy supplied in the form of bibliographic citations by the library. While lists of items should be sent to me regularly throughout the year, it will be important that a final editorial deadline be established. Thus, any items received from the library after January 15 will have to be held over for an entire year.

Since the Checklist is to be published under the auspices of the Department of English, our relationship with the library will be a contractual one. In accordance with your estimates, I have budgeted $2,500 to provide for library research assistance during the coming year. I understand that you will assign a staff member of the library reference department to devote approximately one quarter of his time to searching the literature for items to be included in the Checklist.

While I am anxious that the Checklist be exhaustive, and that we not fail to include every Lawrence item that appears next year, I realize that your man might well devote himself to searching the literature on a full-time basis and still not be able to examine all the sources, especially those in other languages, that might conceivably list items we would want to include. Since we will only be able to pay for a few hours a week of his time, we will have to content ourselves with what he can accomplish in that number of hours. As the person responsible for this project, I feel that I must assure myself that our reference assistant (you see I have already developed a proprietary interest in him) is using his time most effectively and covering the most likely sources of information.

I wonder if you or someone on your staff would prepare an informal memorandum indicating how you plan to approach the project, and send it to me as soon as possible? While I do not expect you to list every bibliography that may be used, I do hope you can make it reasonably detailed. In that way, I can make certain that no potentially important source is being overlooked. Indeed, I shall be interested to learn how a librarian goes about planning a literature search of this kind.

I should add that I have discussed the Checklist and the library's part in it with Vice-President Ellington, and he has given *carte blanche* to proceed as we see fit. The administration is most interested in this as a pilot project, and I, too, hope that it will be only the first of many joint ventures.

Frank Renton, Chief of the Reference Department at the Garonne University Library, sat in the office of the Director of the Library, Dr. Ferguson, reading the above memorandum. When he had finished reading it, Dr. Ferguson said: "Well, Frank, what do you think about this? Can we do it?"

"Forgive me, Dr. Ferguson, I'm rather surprised, that's all. I simply had no idea until I saw this memo that you were planning anything like this with Professor Slater."

"I apologize for springing it on you like this, but, as a matter of fact, it came as something of a surprise to me, too. Let me explain. You have known Ralph Slater almost as long as I have. In fact, you probably know him better than I, because you see more of him."

"Not really. He hasn't spoken to me for almost two years, ever since the time he came in looking for that book on Robert Frost and discovered we had loaned it to another library."

"Oh, yes. That was when he wanted us to ask his permission before we sent anything in the 800 classification out on interlibrary loan."

"Yes. He took it as a personal affront that we would lend anything that was in his field of interest to another library. He's quite a character."

"He certainly is. In any event, the background of the memorandum, briefly, is this. About two months ago, just after classes began in September, the President had his annual social evening for senior faculty and administrative officers at the faculty club. Ralph came up to me during the course of the evening and began talking about how difficult it was for the younger men in the English department to get things published. I agreed that it was a problem because there aren't enough journals in English and American literature to accommodate all of the manuscripts that ambitious young instructors and assistant professors are grinding out these days. Needless to say, I didn't phrase my reply to Slater in quite those terms."

"I'm sure you didn't."

"Frank, long years of administrative experience have taught me never to argue with a man who has no sense of humor, and Ralph Slater doesn't have one. Well, then he began to talk about an idea he had for a series of annotated bibliographies to be published by the English department, each to be edited by one of his protégés. He said he had been trying to convince the junior faculty in his department that bibliographic research was the thing to do, and an excellent way to build up a reputation in scholarly circles. I agreed that we could always use more bibliographies. Then he asked me if the library would ever be interested in 'assisting' in a project of this kind, and I said it seemed quite appropriate to me for a librarian to do this. I pointed out, of course, that work of this kind would have to be financed properly, and that we couldn't just assign a member of the staff to such a project at our expense. He asked me how much time it would take for a reference librarian to do the kind of searching that would be required in order to develop a fairly complete list of everything that was currently being published about a particular author. I think he used James Joyce as an example. I told him I thought it might take five or six hours a week for a trained person to do this. He asked me how much that would cost, and I said I thought about $2,500 a year. Frankly, I didn't take any of this very seriously at the time. In the first place, Slater is notorious for coming up with a scheme that is going to revolutionize the scholarly world today, and then forgetting all about it tomorrow. Nobody takes these ideas of his seriously, including the people in his own department. That's why I didn't even bother to mention it to you at the time. For one thing, I felt sure he'd never get the money to finance it."

"Well, apparently someone takes his ideas seriously, or is at least willing to finance a Lawrence Checklist."

"Apparently so. I'd love to know where he got the money for this. I would guess from his memo that he's got at least $25,000 to put into this Checklist, over a five year period."

"What do you suppose will happen when that money runs out?"

"If you mean do I think that no more issues of the Lawrence Checklist will be published after the money runs out, the answer is no. Slater is shrewd enough to realize that once he's got this thing going, the university can't afford to let it die."

"The university will step in and pay the bill."

"Certainly. If anyone subscribes to it, and people surely will, it will become a matter of institutional prestige, and will have to be continued."

"The memorandum mentions other projects of this kind. I assume by that he means a whole series of annual checklists, each covering a different author."

"Oh, yes. I'm sure that is exactly what Slater has in mind; each one edited by one of his young men, with himself as editor-in-chief. But, for the moment we've only the first one to worry about."

"Why do you suppose he happened to pick Lawrence? Our holdings of Lawrence material are quite adequate, but certainly not outstanding."

"I haven't the faintest notion. You know how often the winds shift in scholarly circles. Maybe Slater expects an upsurge of interest in Lawrence. My own guess is that he's got some young assistant professor over there who's threatening to leave unless he's promoted, and perhaps Slater either can't promote him or doesn't want to. He can toss the fairhaired boy an extra few hundred dollars a year for editing the checklist, and his protégé can get himself a cheap publication at the same time."

"You're probably right. Actually, though, I do think an annotated annual checklist on a major author like Lawrence is a good idea, if it's competently done. Now, I'm sure there are Lawrence checklists in existence, but I don't believe any are done on an annual basis. And, more important, the five and ten year checklists that do come out are almost never annotated. So, in a sense, what he is proposing is rather unique, and ought to fill a need."

"Yes, I agree. This kind of bibliography would be especially useful for a graduate student who didn't specialize in Lawrence, but who had a term paper to do on him."

"And also for a teacher who wasn't a Lawrence specialist, but had to cover Lawrence in a course, and wanted to keep up with the more important things published each year."

"Actually, I rather like the idea of our staff taking part in this project too, although I wish it were being directed by someone who's a little less of a prima donna than Slater. You know how hard I've been pressing to get recognition and faculty rank for our professional staff below the department head level. Taking part in a project of this kind might be quite helpful to us in that respect."

"I agree, and in any event, I assume we have no choice but to take it on."

"Hardly! Slater's got the money, and he's willing to compensate us for the time involved. More important, he's spoken to the vice-president. I think that we're committed to do this. Do you have someone who could handle it?"

"I'll have to think about that a little bit, but I'm sure we can manage it."

"Then I'd like you to take it from here, if you don't mind. Assign someone to the job, have that person work up a memorandum and have a conference with Slater, if you think that would be a good idea, and get the mechanics of the thing set up."

The Garonne University Library is a large one, with holdings of more than a million and a half volumes. The reference collection is of particularly high quality, and includes all of the major current national bibliographies, periodical indexes and subject bibliographies. The library subscribes to nearly six thousand periodicals and serial publications, with foreign language titles especially well represented among its holdings.

• • • • •

Assume that you are a member of the reference staff at the Garonne University Library, and have been assigned the task of working with the English department on the proposed D. H. Lawrence Checklist. The solution to this problem consists of the preparation of a carefully constructed, informal memorandum outlining in some detail a plan for conducting a literature search along the lines indicated in the case study. It should be noted that, although the search is to be conducted on a week-by-week basis, it will be necessary to cover as many relevant sources as possible, without regard for their frequency of publication. Some indication should, perhaps, be given in the memorandum of the degree of completeness of coverage that can be expected. The memorandum may also appropriately incorporate any questions about the Checklist that should be resolved before the work is begun, as well as any suggestions you wish to offer for improvements in the basic plan as it has been outlined by Professor Slater.

8.
A Bibliography
of D. H. Lawrence
Part II
. . . . . .

Approximately four weeks after the events described in the preceding case, Frank Renton looked up from his desk to find Dr. Slater standing in the office doorway.

"Have you a moment, Mr. Renton?"

"Of course, Dr. Slater. Come in, please, and sit down."

"I am sorry to trouble you, and my visit may be needless, but Dr. Ferguson and I have just had a rather lengthy discussion about the Lawrence Checklist and he urged me to stop by and talk with you."

"Of course, the Lawrence Checklist."

"You have heard of it, perhaps? From Dr. Ferguson?"

"Yes. Oh, yes, I have heard of it—from Dr. Ferguson."

"Quite so. Splendid chap, Dr. Ferguson. Very solid. An obvious scholar."

"Dr. Slater, was it about the arrangements for the bibliographic work on the Checklist that Dr. Ferguson suggested you see me?"

"Heavens, no! The bibliographic arrangements were completed quite satisfactorily this afternoon with Dr. Ferguson. All perfectly satisfactory— Dr. Ferguson understands precisely what is required. But I did mention a related matter, with which he suggested you might be in a position to be helpful. Dr. Ferguson tells me you are something of a specialist with journals. Is that correct?"

"Well, every librarian is 'something of a specialist' when it comes to

serials, Dr. Slater. I'm not sure I know much more about them than anybody else in the reference department."

"I see. Well, I confess, it did seem a curious sort of 'specialization'
for anybody to have. However, the question, Mr. . . . ah . . . Mr. Ring-
don . . . is about subscriptions. We in the English department have been
considering how our little bibliographic babe is to be launched on the
waters of 'akademia.' You are evidently familiar with plans for the Checklist. The audience will, of course, be a scholarly one. What size would you
estimate our printing should be for the first issue?"

"Dr. Slater, offhand, I haven't the faintest idea. But I could probably
dig up some figures on the circulation of comparable newsletters, if that
would be of any help to you."

"Actually, that might be quite useful, and I'd be grateful for being
spared the burden of contacting colleagues elsewhere for advice. One never
enjoys appearing naive before one's colleagues in matters of this sort. Also,
we shall be needing some sort of mailing list—any details you might be able
to give us on that would be appreciated."

"Just offhand, I would think there must be directories you could use
as a mailing list. I'd be glad to give that some thought and to see what
I can find out about the circulation of comparable publications to guide
you in planning the size of the initial run. You'd want this fairly soon, I
suppose?"

"I should be most grateful for the information, as soon as you could
get it to me, of course. And there is one other matter which you might
look into, if you have the time. One of my young chaps in the department
has come up with the rather intriguing suggestion that we forego a subscription list for the Checklist. Instead, he suggests that we simply mail
copies of the first volume to what he calls 'likely prospects' with a bill,
and ask them either to pay for it or return the book. Those who pay the
bill automatically receive the next annual issue with a bill, and so on. Chapman claims we'll save enough on billing to more than compensate for any
subscribers who don't pay or return the book. I must say I don't fancy
turning the department office into a billing office, and so I find the suggestion of not keeping a subscription list rather appealing. Chapman says
the science people do it all the time these days with their journals. I
suppose you know all about it?"

"To tell the truth, I've never heard of subscriptions being handled that
way before. But if you'd like, I'll gladly look into it for you."

"Fine. Very grateful to you. I'll have word from you in a few days, then?"

"Certainly, Dr. Slater. As soon as I can get some information together for you."

• • • • •

If you were Mr. Renton, which sources would you consult to bring together the kind of information sought by Dr. Slater? Assuming you decided to send a written report to him, what facts and recommendations would it contain in answer to the several questions he has raised?

9.
A Telephone Question

· · · · · · · · · · · · · · · · · ·

"Reference desk, Miss Waverly speaking."

"Hello?"

"Hello, this is the reference desk."

"Is this the library?"

"Yes, it is."

"The *public* library?"

"Yes, this is the reference desk of the public library. Can I help you?"

"I'm trying to find a book. Can you tell me if the library has it?"

"If you'll give me the author and title, I'll check it for you in the card catalog."

"You have to know who wrote it?"

"Yes, I'll need the author's name or the title before I can look it up in the catalog."

"Do you have any books on marriage?"

"Yes, we do, a good many. Can you tell me which book you're looking for?"

"There are a lot of books on marriage in the library?"

"Yes, quite a few."

"I mean *recent* books. Do you have any that are recent?"

"Yes, we do."

"Could you tell me the names of the recent ones?"

"I'm sorry, I wouldn't be able to do that over the telephone. It would take much too long. The only thing I could suggest is that you come down to the library and check the card catalog yourself."

"Do you have a list of books by their subjects?"

"Yes, we do."

"Could you tell me what you have under 'divorce'?"

"As I said, I couldn't take the time to read the titles under that subject heading to you over the telephone. It would take too long. If you can tell me the particular book you're trying to find, I can look *that* up in the card catalog and see if we have it. Otherwise, I'd just have to suggest you come down to the library and check yourself."

"Can you just tell me what books you have on divorce that are recent? Can you just give me those titles?"

"No, I'm sorry, that would take almost as long as reading all the entries in the card catalog under that subject. I'm afraid we just can't do that over the telephone. Aren't you able to come to the library?"

"Well, it's very hard. I have three children and I don't have a car and I really just can't."

"Could you come in the evening? We're open until ten, Monday through Friday."

"The thing is, I don't want to come all the way down unless you've got the book I'm looking for. It's a new book, I think, and it's about divorce."

"Do you know the name of the author?"

"No, I don't."

"How about the title?"

"Divorce. It's got 'divorce' in the title, I think."

"But you don't remember the *exact* title?"

"No. A friend was telling me about it. It's by a doctor, I know that, and it's about how divorce can be a good thing, you know? I mean this doctor who wrote it says that for certain people, under certain circumstances, divorce can be a very good thing, even for the children. Do you know if you have it?"

"I'm sorry. I don't remember reading anything like that recently. But we buy about 4,000 new books a year here at the library, and I just can't keep up with everything that's new. Have you read the book—is that how you know so much about it?"

"No, my friend told me about it."

"Then couldn't you just call her up and ask her the name of the author? Then call us back and we can tell you if we have it."

"She's in California on vacation with her husband. Besides, she never told me the name of the author, but she did give me the title. I know it had 'divorce' in the title. I'm pretty sure of that. And it's recent. That's why I thought if you could tell me some of the recent books you have on divorce, I'd probably recognize it, if you have it."

"Well, I'm afraid this has taken a good deal of time already, and there may be other people trying to reach the library by telephone, so I hate to tie up the phone any longer. We have only this one line for incoming calls to the reference desk. But hold on just one minute and I'll check the catalog."

Leaving the telephone off the hook at the reference desk, Miss Waverly walked to the card catalog, and returned with the tray covering the *Dib* to *Dju* portion of the alphabet. Her telephone conversation continued as follows:

"I have the catalog entries under 'divorce' in front of me now. I'll read the titles of some of the more recent ones to you, and you stop me if you recognize the one you're looking for. O.K.?"

"Yes."

"O.K. We have *The Way of Divorce* by Baldwin, *The Divorce Handbook* by Haussamen and Guitar, *Divorce and Remarriage* by Pospishil, *Marriage, Divorce, Annulment* by Resnicoff and . . . let me see, recent titles . . . *When Parents Divorce* by Steinzor. Those are the recent titles we have listed under 'divorce'."

"Are any of those by doctors?"

"There's no way to tell from the catalog. It just gives the name of the author, not his titles or degrees. Do you recognize any of the titles I read?"

"I don't think so. A couple of them sounded like they might be it. I'm not sure. Is there any other way I could go about finding it? How about calling a bookstore?"

"You might try that."

"Can you suggest one in town I could call?"

"No, we couldn't recommend a particular bookstore to you."

"Which one does the library use?"

"We don't buy our books through a bookstore. We buy from a dealer or direct from the publisher. But you might try calling Rochester's, they have about the largest stock of any of the local stores."

"Do they carry paperbacks?"

"Is the book you're looking for a paperback?"

"Yes."

"Oh, for heavens sake! If you'd told me that in the first place, it would have saved both of us a lot of time. The library has only a few paperback books, mostly fiction, and those are not cataloged."

"I'm sorry. I guess you can't help me, then."

"No, I'm afraid we can't. Goodbye."

Miss Waverly hung up the telephone in disgust and returned the tray to the card catalog, mumbling under her breath about the mental short-comings of the human race in general, and of those who ask telephone reference questions in particular.

Phyllis Waverly is one of three members of the professional staff of the reference department at the Moselle Public Library which serves a suburban community of 88,000 people near one of the largest cities in the country. The library is strong, well-supported and adequately staffed. It enjoys an excellent reputation, being considered one of the finest public libraries in the state and region in which it is located. The reference collection, comprising over 1,000 volumes, contains all the standard titles one would expect to find in a good medium-sized public library system, with particular depth in business, art and music. The department has a budget of approximately $2,500 a year for the purchase of new reference books, exclusive of subscriptions to bibliographies and indexes, which are carried in the periodicals budget. New titles and replacements are carefully selected from books recommended in such sources as *The Booklist and Subscription Books Bulletin, Choice, Library Journal* and the "Standard Catalog" series. The reference collection is supplemented by extensive files of pamphlets and government documents, subscriptions to 350 current periodicals and a general book collection of nearly 150,000 volumes. All telephone reference service is handled at the general reference desk, which is located near the card catalog and the reference collection.

● ● ● ● ●

How would you analyze and evaluate the reference interview which Miss Waverly conducted in this case study? In what respects do you feel the inquiry was well handled? What specific suggestions, if any, can you make that might have resulted in improved communication in this instance?

Given the circumstances, do you feel that this inquiry was dealt with in a satisfactory manner? In Miss Waverly's place, how would you have resolved the caller's problem? On the basis of the information given, would it have been possible to have identified the particular book which was being sought? If so, what is the book?

In a situation of this kind, do you feel that a patron who telephones the library requesting information has the right to expect as much by way of time and professional assistance as was given the inquirer in this case? More?

10.
Restricted Reference Sources

· ·

Ivywild College is a small, liberal arts institution for women, located near a rural community in southern New England. Founded eighty-five years ago as a non-sectarian "academy for young ladies," Ivywild has pioneered in experimental programs in higher education for women. In recent years, particular emphasis has been placed on what the Ivywild catalog describes as "experience in the creative arts." Painting, sculpture, music and the dance are a part of the Ivywild way of life, and consume much of the time and interest of its 440 undergraduate women.

The Ivywild faculty is large in terms of the total enrollment, numbering forty-seven full time and twenty-two part time instructors. Although the college offers no graduate work, and is located far from major metropolitan areas, Ivywild has been successful in attracting and retaining a faculty of unusual distinction. Salaries are high, conditions of tenure pleasant, and the administration both effective and unobtrusive. These factors combine to produce an environment that has proved particularly attractive to mature men and women who have made scholarly reputations elsewhere.

The college library boasts a small, but well-chosen collection of about 100,000 volumes that is adequate to meet most instructional needs. The library participates in a cooperative acquisitions program with several other small colleges in the immediate area, and makes imaginative use of inter-library loan and micro-reproductions to supplement local resources. Under the guidance of its energetic director, Joseph Loudon, the library has achieved an enviable reputation for prompt and efficient service to the whole college community, and enjoys particularly happy relationships with the faculty. The library building is attractive, and as a result of a recently completed addition, sufficiently spacious to house all of the college's book resources under one roof, as well as to provide a phonograph listening lounge, a handsomely appointed browsing room, music practice rooms and a language laboratory.

Evelyn Bishop has been assistant librarian at Ivywild for the past six months, following her graduation from library school. She is young, personable, and eager to please, and has made an excellent impression on all those with whom she has come into contact thus far at the college. Since the library staff is small, Miss Bishop's duties are many and varied. She has particular responsibility for the library's public services, including reference and circulation. The circulation desk is staffed by part-time student workers, under the immediate supervision of Miss Warren, an experienced clerical assistant, so that only the most general kind of supervision is required.

One morning, as Miss Bishop was working at the reference desk, she had a telephone call from Dr. Bartow, Chairman of the Psychology Department, who asked if he might stop by and talk with her that morning. The reply was affirmative, and in due course Dr. Bartow appeared, carrying two slim, yellow volumes under his arm.

DR. BARTOW: "Miss Bishop, I have a small problem here. I'm not quite sure if this is in your line or not, but Margaret Warren suggested that you would be the person to talk to. Let me begin by confessing that, although I've been around Ivywild for more years than I like to remember, I'm afraid that I'm abysmally ignorant about some aspects of the library. Do you have any sort of restricted area here, a closed shelf where books can be kept, so that their use can be controlled?"

MISS BISHOP: "Well, we have a small rare book area, where we also keep a good deal of college archival material, and anything that is particularly valuable or unusual goes in there. Also, there is a closed reserve area behind the circulation desk for books that are in great demand. Otherwise, the whole collection is on open shelves."

DR. BARTOW: "That area behind the circulation desk—those books are, of course, available to students working there?"

MISS BISHOP: "Yes, they would be."

DR. BARTOW: "I'm afraid that wouldn't do. How about the rare book room? Can students get in there?"

MISS BISHOP: "No, never. Only people on the full-time staff have keys."

DR. BARTOW: "The rare book room would seem to be the answer, then. How does one go about having books placed there?"

MISS BISHOP: "Are these the books you have in mind? May I see them?"

Dr. Bartow handed the two books that he had been carrying to Miss Bishop, who examined them briefly. The two volumes are described bibliographically as follows:

Rorschach, Hermann. *Psychodiagnostik: methodik und ergebnisse eines wahrnehmungsdiagnostischen experiments; textband.* (Arbeiten zur angewandten psychiatrie, bd. II.) Bern, Verlag Hans Huber, 1937. 256 pp.

Rorschach, Hermann. *Psychodiagnostik; tafeln.* Bern, Verlag Hans Huber, n.d. (10 plates on stiff boards.)

DR. BARTOW: "You perhaps are not familiar with these, but I'm sure you know the Rorschach Test."

MISS BISHOP: "Yes, I do."

DR. BARTOW: "These are the actual diagnostic plates—the ink-blots, if you will—and the Rorschach manual for interpretation. As you can see, the books belong to the library, but for some years now I have kept them in my office because I was afraid to leave them any place where students could get hold of them. But since they do belong to the library, I think perhaps they should be kept in your rare book area, where I and others of the faculty could get at them when they are needed."

MISS BISHOP: "Well, these are reference books. Do you mean that they shouldn't be in the library except on a closed shelf?"

DR. BARTOW: "Not exactly, but we have something of an unusual situation at Ivywild. As you may know, psychology is a particularly popular subject here. Quite often, girls take psychology for what are, perhaps, the wrong reasons."

MISS BISHOP: "How do you mean?"

DR. BARTOW: "Well, perhaps it's just in the nature of the college, but for some reason we attract a pretty high percentage of girls who are terribly intense, very creative, often more than slightly maladjusted, and sometimes bright enough to realize this. These people gravitate to psychology courses; I suppose, in the hope of finding some answer to their own emotional problems. This is not a bad thing, in itself, because sometimes we can spot a person of this kind, and see that she gets proper psychiatric help, if she needs it. Now, of course, I don't mean for a moment to suggest that all, or even a majority of our students are in this situation, but a fair number are, to one degree or another. My point merely is that the Rorschach Test is a clinical technique, and that I think it's terribly dangerous, especially these days, for untrained and immature people to be fooling around with it. Before you know it, some student will be trying to administer the test to herself, and drawing all sorts of incorrect conclusions. Also, I should point out that the Rorschach technique would be useless as a diagnostic method if the subject had had access to this book and plates. So, unless the library can keep these books under lock and key, and out of the hands of students, I think we'll have to find some other way to handle them."

MISS BISHOP: "Well, of course, I can understand your concern, and these could perfectly well be kept with our rare books. But they would be listed in the card catalog. What do you suggest we do when students ask for them?"

DR. BARTOW: "Tell them 'no!' If any student objects to this, I'll take responsibility for it. Would this be all right?"

MISS BISHOP: "I guess we could handle the books in that way. Why don't you just leave them with me now?"

DR. BARTOW: "Fine! And, thanks very much."

The books remained on the reference desk throughout the rest of the morning, and the early afternoon; each time that Miss Bishop glanced at them, she felt vaguely uneasy about her conversation with Dr. Bartow. She wondered if perhaps this might not set a poor precedent, and it occurred to her that it might be well to raise the question with Mr. Loudon. On the other hand, it seemed such a small matter as hardly to merit the attention of the director.

Later that afternoon, Miss Bishop found herself in Mr. Loudon's office on other business, and decided to raise the question of library policy in restricting reference use of books, using the Rorschach book as an example. Mr. Loudon indicated interest, and Miss Bishop soon found herself recounting the conversation with Dr. Bartow. After Miss Bishop had finished her recital of the morning's events, Mr. Loudon said:

"Evelyn, I'm just not sure about all this. Now, please understand, I'm not being critical of the way you handled Dr. Bartow. Certainly, the last thing that we want to do is to antagonize him, especially over what is really a very small matter. I think that if I'd been in your place, I'd have responded in about the same way. On the other hand, this raises some rather fundamental questions in my mind and, I suspect, in yours too, or we wouldn't be talking about it. I almost wonder if it wouldn't be better to withdraw these books from the collection, and just give them to the Psychology Department, and let them handle them in any way that they want? I'll tell you what. I'd like to look at the books myself. Let me mull this over, look at the books, and then perhaps we can talk further about it."

· · · · ·

Is there anything unreasonable or improper about Dr. Bartow's request that the Rorschach books not be placed on the open shelves in the college library? Do you agree with the way in which Miss Bishop handled the problem? What further action, if any, should Mr. Loudon take? Are the concepts of freedom of access to information which are generally accepted by the library profession applicable in the case of these particular books? If so, is it possible to reconcile these concepts with the library's acceptance of Dr. Bartow's recommendation? How do you evaluate Mr. Loudon's suggestion that the books be given to the Psychology Department?

11.
Financial Research

· · · · · · · · · · · · · · ·

"Are you Mr. Fordyce?" Ralph Fordyce, Head Librarian of the Orinoco Public Library, looked up from his desk to greet an attractive young woman who stood somewhat hesitantly in the doorway of his office, which was located just off the main reading room of the small suburban library.

"Yes, I am. Come in, please and sit down. Is there something I can do to help you?"

"I'm not sure, but the lady at the desk said I should speak to you. I'm Mrs. Litchfield. I hate to bother you, but I've been trying to find some information and somebody told me I ought to try looking it up in the library. You see, we're new in town. My husband and I are from the midwest, but we like New England very much. My husband is an engineer with Bethel. We've only been married a year, and we've been living here since just after we were married. I've never been to your library before today. Jim reads a lot, but all engineering things; and I'm afraid I'm not much of a reader."

"Well, I'm glad you discovered the library. You know, the library isn't here just to provide for people who are 'readers.' That was its whole problem before I came here, just four months ago. Miss Florence, who was my predecessor, operated under what we call the 'demand theory' in book selection, and just bought what people who were already using the library asked for. The result is that in the adult book collection we've got lots of light fiction—mystery stories and that kind of thing—plus shelves of multiple copies of old best sellers, but not too much else. However, we are trying to build up the collections, and I want the adults in Orinoco to start thinking of the library as more than just a place to come when they're looking for recreational reading. I'd like to make this library into a real community information center, so whoever told you that this was the place to look for information had the right idea."

"That's very nice of you, Mr. Fordyce, really. Now I don't feel so guilty about bothering you. I did look through a few books, but I didn't have any luck at all. Probably I'm just stupid and don't know where to look."

"Tell me what it is you're trying to find."

"I'm looking for something on interest."

"Interest? You mean, like interest on a loan?"

"No, on a mortgage."

"You want to find out how much interest you'd have to pay on a mortgage, is that it?"

"No, that's not it exactly. It's sort of hard to explain because I don't really understand it myself. But the thing is this. We're going to buy a house here in town. We've never owned a house before, so mortgages and that kind of thing are all new and confusing to us. The funny thing is, my husband, being an engineer, is a lot better at math than I am. But, I just can't get him to sit down and figure this out. He's the kind of person who never bothers to count his change, if you know what I mean. Well, somebody in a family has to pay attention to these things, don't you agree?"

"Sure. And you're elected, I guess?"

"I guess so. But to get to the point about interest on the mortgage. After we found the house we wanted, we went and talked yesterday with the man at the bank. He explained about the interest and the insurance, and all that, and what the monthly payments would be. Of course, my husband didn't pay the least bit of attention to the details, but I got it all written down. Anyway, last night, I sat down at home and went over and over those figures, and I just couldn't get them to come out right."

"How do you mean, 'come out right'?"

"I mean the interest doesn't come out right. It looks to me like we're paying several hundred dollars more to the bank, over the period of the mortgage, than we should be paying. And the faster the mortgage is paid off, the more we wind up paying."

"Well, I understand about paying more than the face value of the mortgage. That, of course, is because of the interest and the insurance."

"No, that's what I thought at first too. But even allowing for interest and insurance and taxes—I worked it all out very carefully, and used the figures the man at the bank gave us—it still comes out that we're paying too much. Do you follow me?"

"No, I'm not sure I do."

"I didn't understand it either, so this morning I went back and talked to the man at the bank again, because it just seemed to me that we would be paying over nine percent interest instead of eight and a half percent, the way they'd told us. Anyway, I'm even more confused after talking to the man at the bank. He said it's because of the 'points,' and that what it actually means is not that we pay more interest, but that we receive less than the actual amount of the mortgage. Because of the 'points.' Maybe you understand about 'points' but I certainly don't."

"Did they explain it to you at the bank?"

"Well, in a way, they did. But I'm the kind of person who just doesn't understand a thing completely unless I can take it home and sit down and work it out for myself. That's why I decided to come down to the library, and see if I could get a book that would explain about mortgages and points, and all that. Do you know if you have anything like that? I looked through some books, but I couldn't find it."

"The truth is, Mrs. Litchfield, our reference collection is sort of limited, but why don't we take a look and see what we can find?"

"Oh, I hate to bother you. You must be busy. If you'll just tell me where to look it up, I can do that myself."

"I'm afraid finances are something of a mystery to me, too. Offhand, I wouldn't be able to tell you where to look. But let's see what we can find together."

Mr. Fordyce devoted the next forty-five minutes to searching the library's limited holdings on the subject of mortgage rates and the point system. He quickly worked his way through the small number of titles on the reference shelves which he felt might contain the sort of explanation Mrs. Litchfield was seeking. He checked index references under the headings "interest," "mortgage" and "points" in the *World Almanac*, the *Information Please Almanac*, the *Economic Almanac* and all five of the general encyclopedias, but was unable to locate any relevant information. A search of the card catalog under the heading "finance" turned up a half dozen titles in the general collection dealing with various aspects of personal and family money management. He discovered that all of these were several years out of date, and none contained any explanation of the point system as it affected mortgage rates. Rather discouraged, he returned to the table in the reference room where Mrs. Litchfield was waiting to report his lack of success.

"Mrs. Litchfield, I just can't seem to find anything in our collection relating to mortgages that will give you what you want. We don't seem to have anything detailed enough, or for that matter, up to date enough. This is the kind of frustrating thing that has been happening to me every couple of days for the last four months here. We'll get all the gaps in the collection filled eventually, but that doesn't do you much good right now, does it?"

"No, I guess not. Well, thanks anyway for taking the time."

"Say, wait a minute! I just had an idea. One of our trustees, George de Quincy, is the manager of the Orinoco Savings and Loan. I'll bet he could tell us where to get the information on the point system. If it's in print someplace, I could probably get it for you in a couple of days through the regional library. Let me call him."

"I . . . I'd really rather that you didn't. Why don't we just let it go?"

"It's no trouble, Mrs. Litchfield. I'd be glad to. And I'm sure George wouldn't mind helping out. He's really a very good trustee."

"I'm sure he is, but, you see, Mr. de Quincy is the man I talked to at the bank this morning. And I wouldn't want him to know that I came down here to ask you about this."

"Oh, I understand. The thing is though, I really can't think of any other way to locate what you want. If George could tell me what book has information on interest rates and the point system, I'd know what to ask for from the regional. Without a specific title, the regional can't be much help to us. But look, why don't I just raise the question with him? I don't have to tell him who it is that's asking. Wouldn't that be all right?"

With some reluctance, Mrs. Litchfield agreed and she followed Mr. Fordyce into his office, where he quickly reached George de Quincy by telephone at the Orinoco Savings and Loan Association. Their telephone conversation was as follows:

"George, this is Ralph Fordyce calling."

"How are you Ralph? What's up?"

"Relax, George. No trustee-type problem. Just a request for some information that I thought you'd be able to put your finger on rather quickly for me."

"Sure, if I can help. Is it something for the library?"

"Yes, it is. We've had a request for information on mortgage interest rates as they're affected by what's called the point system. I suppose you know all about that?"

"About points? Oh, yes, I do."

"What is this point thing all about, George?"

"Well, very briefly, it's one percent of the face value of a mortgage. When a person borrows from a bank like ours on a home mortgage, for example, they're charged a given number of points and that's deducted from the amount the borrower receives."

"It's like additional interest, then?"

"No, not really. It doesn't affect the interest rate."

"George, what I'm really after is some book or pamphlet that would provide a layman with a simple explanation of this point system and an indication of how it affects the amount of money that has to be repaid on a mortgage. Could you suggest a source on this?"

"Ralph, this is a very complicated matter that people in my business spend years learning. I'd suggest you refer whoever wants this information directly to the lending officer at his bank. Is this by any chance one of our customers?"

"I . . . I really don't know, George."

"Is it someone local?"

"I . . . guess so. I'm really not sure. There's nothing in print, then?"

"Well, we use the Carleton tables here at the bank, but they're a restricted publication, I'm certain. For one thing, they're only available to banks, I believe, and for another, they'd be meaningless to a layman. But again, Ralph, I'd simply urge as strongly as I can that the library not, under any circumstances, attempt to supply this kind of information to anybody. This is a very complex matter which should be handled by a professional, and where a layman could be seriously misled and misinformed if he were simply handed a set of interest rate tables without a very careful, informed, personal explanation. I just don't think this is any kind of area for the library to be getting into."

Mr. de Quincy's final statement was uttered with such a tone of finality and strong conviction that it was clear to Mr. Fordyce that it would be useless to pursue the question further with him. Without indicating how he intended to dispose of the matter, Mr. Fordyce merely terminated the telephone conversation with his trustee as gracefully as he could.

• • • • •

Assuming that you were Mr. Fordyce, what would you say to Mrs.

Litchfield at this point? Would you continue to attempt to locate the information she is seeking? Where can a simple, clear and accurate explanation of the effect of mortgage points on interest rates be found? Would it be available in sources likely to be found in the collections of the Orinoco Public Library?

How would you evaluate Mr. Fordyce's handling of the reference interview in this instance? Of the initial search through library materials? Were any promising types of sources, or specific sources, overlooked? Had you been Mr. Fordyce, would you have suggested calling Mr. de Quincy as he did and at the point that he did? How would you, in Fordyce's place, have responded to Mr. de Quincy's question about the identity of the inquirer?

12.
Family Guidance
. . . .

"Ladies and Gentlemen, since it's after eight and all members of the Board of Trustees are present, I'm going to suggest we begin the meeting."

The speaker was Arthur Rantoul, Chairman of the Board of Trustees of the Warta Public Library. His audience comprised five fellow members of the Board, Mrs. Carmi, Mrs. Millen, Mr. Sebring, Mr. Bartow, and Mr. Shelton, as well as the director of the Warta Public Library, Frank Ormond, and the head of the reference department, Margaret Jesup. Mr. Rantoul continued:

"To begin, I'd like to explain, particularly for the benefit of Mrs. Millen, our newly appointed member, and Chris Sebring, who's probably wondering, since he's been out of town for three weeks, just why I called this emergency meeting of the Board and why I've asked Miss Jesup to be present. I hope the other members of the Board and the librarians will be patient, and I promise to try to be brief.

"I think we're all familiar with the controversy that's been going on in town for the last year or two over sex education in the schools. What's been happening here is, as I understand it, very much a reflection of what's going on all over the country, because sex education or family guidance or whatever you want to call it has evidently become a fashionable subject for schools to teach. Many people, many parents, many church groups and other groups, have very strong feelings against the schools' getting into this subject. I understand that in a number of cities, pressure from parents and the public has been so great that the schools have had to stop it.

"Those of us who know Warta, who've lived here all our lives, have not, I think, been surprised at the way various individuals and groups in

52

the community have responded to the attempt to introduce sex education into the Warta schools. You all read the local papers, and I'm sure you know this is the biggest and most bitter controversy to have hit this town in years. If you've seen the stories, editorials and letters that have been running in the *Herald* over the last year, you must realize that some of it has been pretty nasty. But unless you've attended a school board meeting recently, and I think I'm perhaps the only person here who has, I don't think you can appreciate just how emotional and downright ugly this thing has become. I've been to two recent meetings of the school board, just as an interested citizen, and I've seen members of the board, the superintendent and individual teachers who are involved in the sex education program simply vilified publicly by those people who oppose it. They've been called everything from 'communists' to 'perverts.' Even the *Herald*, which certainly isn't finicky in reporting local politics, can't print what really has been going on at those meetings. Not to mention the letters and telephone calls which some of us have gotten a taste of in the last two weeks.

"As I understand it, the library's involvement in this stems from a reading list on sex education which was prepared and distributed by our reference department, without, I think, the advance knowledge of the library director, and certainly without the knowledge of the Board. I am going to ask Mr. Ormond and Miss Jesup to enlighten the Board about this in just a moment, but before I do, let me say that I have had a number of letters and telephone calls from people in town since this reading list was made available in the library two weeks ago, and particularly since it was published in the *Herald* last week. I believe that Mrs. Carmi has been contacted as well, have you not?"

MRS. CARMI: "Yes, I'm afraid I have had a number of telephone calls, some of which have been extremely disturbing, as have some of the letters I've received."

MR. SEBRING: "Arthur, who is it that's calling you and Sarah and writing you letters, and what the devil is it they're objecting to?"

MR. RANTOUL: "Some are connected with the group called Citizens for Parental Rights, which I believe is Monsignor Stockton's organization. Others are simply individual parents who have been fighting sex education in the schools from its inception, and who object violently to the public library's taking sides on this issue. To them, the library is in the position of being in league with the school department in promoting a program which a sizeable part of this community is strongly opposed to."

MR. SEBRING: "How have you and Sarah responded to the calls and letters?"

MRS. CARMI: "I have referred any that I have received to Mr. Rantoul as our chairman. I do have very strong personal feelings about this situation, but before expressing them I would like to hear first from our library director."

MR. RANTOUL: "To answer your question, Chris, as Chairman of the Board, I have taken it upon myself to declare our regularly scheduled meeting next Thursday evening an open meeting, to be held in the library auditorium, to which all interested groups and individuals who are concerned about the library's involvement in the school sex education program will be invited and given an opportunity to be heard."

MR. SEBRING: "Wow! Sounds like we're in for it next Thursday night."

MR. RANTOUL: "I hope not, Chris, but I felt I had no alternative. These people are citizens and taxpayers who are unhappy about something that has been done in the name of the library and who have brought their complaints directly to the Board. I think we have no alternative but to invite them to meet with us and express their views. We serve on this Board as representatives of the people of Warta, to give the people the kind of public library they want. Personally, I have no position on the matter of sex education in the schools. I am impressed by the arguments on both sides. The people who oppose it, and who are incensed at the library's having taken a position on it by issuing this booklist, are entitled to a hearing before the Board, in my opinion. We may not like the tactics being used, but all people have a right to express their opinions. In any event, my purpose in calling tonight's meeting was to establish the facts and give the Board an opportunity to prepare itself for next Thursday's meeting. To this end, I'd like to call on our director to explain how the reading list on sex education came to be issued."

MR. ORMOND: "I would just like to say to the Board that I am very sorry this meeting tonight was necessary and that you have been harassed individually in this way. I'm sure the aim of the reference department in doing the list was to make a positive contribution toward reducing community tensions, but it would seem the result has been just the opposite. Since the booklist was a project of the reference department, I'd like Miss Jesup to explain the background of it."

MISS JESUP: "Well, very briefly, shortly after I came to work at the library about two years ago, the family guidance courses were first being planned, and Mr. Lombard, who was in charge of the pilot program at the junior high school where it was introduced, came to me for help in locating books and pamphlets for use both by teachers and students. As you may know, that particular junior high school does not have a school librarian, nor for that matter much by way of a school library. Over the past two years, the reference department has done a good deal of bibliographic work for Mr. Lombard, to help him in developing the family guidance curriculum on a systematic basis. The bibliography on sex education was actually taken from a much longer list of books, articles, pamphlets and audio-visual materials which we prepared with Mr. Lombard for teachers to use. When it was finished, the schools used it as a buying list for their central curriculum collection and the public library bought many of the items as well, so that they would be available for parents to use. In my opinion, much of the opposition to the family guidance program comes from parents who aren't prepared to discuss these matters with their children or to handle the questions that children bring home. Since the library has so much material that would be helpful to parents, it seemed a good idea to bring this to the attention of the public through the booklist. In case any of you have not seen it, I've brought copies with me."

At this point, Miss Jesup handed around copies of an annotated list of approximately thirty titles relating to sex education. The attractively printed list carried the title "Family Living: Useful Books and Pamphlets for Parents in the Warta Public Library" with a note indicating that it had been "prepared with the assistance of Henry C. Lombard, Coordinator of the Family Guidance Program, Warta Public Schools for use by parents of children enrolled in the Family Guidance curriculum." Mrs. Millen, a newly appointed member of the Board, was the first to speak:

"Mr. Chairman, you must forgive my ignorance, but as a new member I want to be sure I have all the facts clear in my own mind. Miss Jesup, did you say that the school department asked the library to publish this reading list?"

MISS JESUP: "No, compiling and publishing this list was entirely the library's idea—the reference department's idea, actually. But Mr. Lombard was very enthusiastic about it, because of all the problems he's been having with parents, and I understand the superintendent of schools was quite pleased as well, especially when the *Herald* decided to run it."

MR. SHELTON: "How did the list come to appear in the *Herald*, does anyone know?"

MISS JESUP: "Sure, I sent it to them."

MRS. MILLEN: "Mr. Chairman, I do have one or two other questions, if I may. Am I correct in understanding from what has been said previously, Mr. Ormond, that you did not consult with the Board or advise them in advance that you intended to publish this list?"

MR. RANTOUL: "I am very certain that the Board had no advance knowledge of this. The first I heard of it was the day it appeared in the *Herald*. I had a telephone call from a very irate man who asked me if I endorsed teaching methods of sexual intercourse to elementary school children."

MR. ORMOND: "I had intended to report publication of the list to the Board at the regular monthly meeting next week, Mrs. Millen. I do that as a regular thing at every Board meeting, to keep the Board informed of what the library is doing."

MRS. MILLEN: "Did the list have your approval, Mr. Ormond?"

MR. ORMOND: "Well, in point of fact . . ."

MISS JESUP: "Forgive me for interrupting, but I would like the Board to understand that I take full responsibility for the preparation and publication of this booklist. I did not ask Mr. Ormond's permission before arranging to have it printed, although I hope he would have approved it. I have been given to understand by Mr. Ormond that I am in charge of the reference department. One of the normal functions of a reference department is the preparation of booklists. We publish a half dozen or more every year. I am given a budget for this, and as long as I don't exceed that budget, I feel free to simply go ahead and issue lists like this without any prior approval."

MR. ORMOND: "What Miss Jesup says is true. This is the way we operate with the department heads."

MR. RANTOUL: "Let me interject just one comment here. Miss Jesup, you may be quite prepared, as you suggested, to 'take full responsibility for this booklist' but as a matter of fact, that is not within your power. I think you and every member of the library staff must understand that it is the Board and Mr. Ormond, who are responsible for everything that is said or done in the name of the library. Now, let me direct a question of my own to Mr. Ormond. Frank, I don't mean to embarrass you by this, but for my own information and the Board's, I would like to know this. If Miss Jesup had consulted with you before undertaking to publish this booklist, would you have approved it?"

MR. ORMOND: "Arthur, with all due respect, I think that's beside the point. What's done is done. Naturally, I support my staff in anything of this kind. I must!"

MRS. CARMI: "Mr. Chairman, I think Mr. Ormond should answer your question. I think this Board has a right to know. Do you think it was wise for the library to publish this list at this time?"

MR. ORMOND: "To be quite honest, I'm not completely sure that it was. But, as I said before, I have every confidence in the professional judgment of the library staff—in Miss Jesup's judgment—and I feel we must support the staff in these matters."

MRS. CARMI: "Mr. Ormond, I agree completely with your suggestion that publication of this sex instruction reading list was unwise. In fact, I feel it was a most serious error of judgment on Miss Jesup's part. Let me make it quite clear that I am unalterably opposed to the schools' offering this kind of instruction to my children or anybody else's children. As a trustee of the library, I have felt bound to remain silent publicly on the matter, because the library does not and cannot take sides on controversial issues, a fact that I think both Mr. Ormond and especially Miss Jesup have apparently forgotten. I consider the adoption of the family guidance curriculum a tragic error for which our children are paying a terrible price. Do you know that in the past two years there have been over two dozen junior high school girls in this city who have had to drop out of school because of pregnancy? That is just part of the price of teaching sexual intercourse to twelve-year-olds.

"But the real issue here, as I see it, is that the library is taking a public position by identifying itself with the school department in supporting this program. Publishing and distributing this reading list in the name of the Warta Public Library was wrong, because it involves the library in a community controversy."

MR. BARTOW: "Sarah, I don't agree with your personal opinions on sex education in the schools, but I do think you have a point about not getting the library involved in it. Look, we've got a bond issue for an addition to the central building coming up next year. This is no time to antagonize any segment of the voters unnecessarily. There are a lot of people in town who are going to jump all over the library for getting involved in this, and they're right. It's none of the library's business. This is between the school board and the community. If ever there was a time to stay neutral, this was it. I'm afraid, Miss Jesup, that you've gotten us up to the knees in somebody else's mudpuddle."

MISS JESUP: "I'd like to say just one thing in reply to what's been said. I disagree completely with the notion that the library should remain silent on controversial issues. The job of the public library is to educate the community, and you can't educate people by remaining silent. We must have sound programs of sex education in the schools and the Warta Family Guidance program is considered a model for other school systems in the state. To my mind, the public library has a clear and urgent responsibility and obligation to dispel ignorance and misunderstanding in the community which it serves. With all due respect to the Board, if you do not understand this, I think you had better reread the ALA *Standards* and find out what a public library is all about."

MR. RANTOUL: "Ladies and gentlemen, this discussion has been underway for some time, and since this is an executive session, I believe that Miss Jesup may be excused at this point, with our thanks, so the Board can proceed with its deliberations. I'm also going to suggest a short recess at this stage to give all of us a chance to cool off a bit. Mrs. Carmi, did you want to say something further before we take a break?"

MRS. CARMI: "Mr. Chairman, I am quite agreeble to the idea of a short recess. Before Miss Jesup leaves, I want to say that when we reconvene, I intend to offer a motion that the Board go on record tonight as reaffirming the library's traditional position of complete neutrality on controversial issues by instructing Mr. Ormond to withdraw the reading list on sex education from circulation. I shall move that he and the staff be further instructed to submit all lists of this kind, in future, to the Board for approval before they are published or released to the news media. Miss Jesup has been quite frank in stating her views to this Board, and as a member of the Board, I want to be equally frank with her."

At this point, Mr. Rantoul indicated that the Board would stand in recess for twenty mintues.

Warta is a city of 111,000 people, one third of whom are second or third generation Americans of middle-European origin. Approximately ten percent of the population is Black or Spanish-speaking. Steelmaking and related heavy industry predominate in the economic life of the city, employing over forty percent of the total work force. The median number of school years completed for the entire population of the city is 11.2. Warta has been plagued for two decades by a corrupt municipal government, deteriorating housing, heavy out-migration of upper and middle income groups, loss of local industry, high unemployment and a declining tax base. The public library has struggled to maintain services and support in the face of rising costs, diminishing circulation, and general public indifference.

• • • • •

Do you feel that the director and/or trustees of the library should have been consulted prior to publication of the sex education reading list? Do you agree with the opinion expressed by some trustees that publication of the list, in its present form, constitutes taking a position on a controversial issue? Do you agree with Miss Jesup that the public library should express itself on this kind of controversial issue in order to meet its responsibilities to the community as an educational agency?

How would you comment on the conduct of Mr. Ormond and Miss Jesup during the board meeting? If you were in Mr. Ormond's place, what position would you take with respect to Mrs. Carmi's proposed motion? What other alternatives are open to the trustees at this point?

13.
Help for
the Handicapped
· · · · · · · · · · · · ·

"Excuse me, are you Ruth Ellsworth?"

"Yes, I am."

"Miss Ellsworth, I'm Jim Brewer from the West End Family Service Center. We're a social service agency working in the inner city. I got your name from Margaret Amherst at the United Fund. She said you'd helped them several times, and she thought you might be able to help me find some material for a young man I'm working with over in my neighborhood."

"I'll certainly be glad to try, if it's something that's in the library. Fortunately you've come in at a time when the reference desk isn't very busy. Why don't we sit down over here, where I can keep an eye on the desk and the phone, and you can tell me what it is you're looking for."

"We have a family that the agency has been working with for about six or seven years, a working mother and two sons. It's an absentee father situation. The oldest son is in the Army. The mother first came to us six years ago, when the younger son, George, got into trouble at school. You know—truancy, gangs, drinking, drugs—the usual sort of thing for a fifteen-year-old in our neighborhood. It turned out, when we began to work with George, that he was an extremely bright kid who was simply bored with school. He'd had some bad counseling and had gotten into a non-academic program that didn't aim to do much more than keep him off the street until he turned seventeen. To make a long story short, we confirmed by testing that he had a very high I.Q., and managed to get him into a good prep school, and subsequently into the state university. He was getting along beautifully until about a year and a half ago when he fractured his spine in a diving accident. He was hospitalized for over fourteen months, and is now paralyzed from the waist down."

"How dreadful. Is he at home now?"

"Yes, he was discharged from City Hospital about five months ago. He would be able to get around in a wheelchair, if he wanted to. His major problem at this point, I think, is psychological. He just seems to have given up on everything and everybody, including himself and his future, and is full of self-pity. But lately, I've gotten him interested in the idea of doing some writing."

"Writing?"

"Before the accident, George was majoring in creative writing. His chief interest was poetry. But poetry isn't much of a career, as you know. The thought I had, however, was that he might be able to earn some money by writing current events articles for magazines. I have a friend who is a freelance writer, works right out of his own home, and makes a nice income writing factual articles for all kinds of magazines. George is very bright, and extremely interested in and well informed about current events. In fact, about all he's done for the last few months is read every newspaper and magazine he can get his hands on. A couple of weeks ago, he and I were discussing a piece he'd seen in the paper about how the federal government is spending large amounts of money every year to try to get people to quit smoking while at the same time a different branch of the government is spending even more money to subsidize the tobacco industry. I suggested to George that there must be a lot of similar examples of two or more agencies spending federal government money at cross purposes to one another. The Agriculture Department, for example, funding research on how to grow more of a particular crop at the same time as it buys up surplus stocks of the same crop at government expense so the farmers won't go broke."

"Yes, I imagine there must be a good deal of that kind of thing among federal agencies."

"Right. Anyway, I've got George interested in trying to write an article on just that subject. My writer friend has offered to give us the names of magazines that might be interested in an article like this, if George can get it written. I'll tell you, this is the first glimmer of light I've seen with this boy in many a month, the first time I've gotten him to even think about putting his life back together again. Miss Ellsworth, if this boy could possibly do this article and sell it to a magazine, it would be a tremendous

thing for him right now. He can write, that I know. And he's really interested in this subject. The problem is, he has no way to get at source
material. He needs books, articles, pamphlets, statistics, that sort of thing,
as a basis for his article."

"And there's no way he could come to the library to do this research,
I suppose."

"Exactly. For one thing, it would simply be impossible for a person
in a wheelchair to get up the steps into this building. But even beyond that,
this family lives in a third floor walkup. Now I'm prepared to be George's
legs, but what I am not able to do is the kind of library research that he
needs. I don't have the time, and I just don't know how to dig out the
source material. That's why I'm here this morning. I want to know if the
public library can put together some source material on the use of federal
funds for antithetical purposes. We need factual material that would serve
as the basis of an article for a popular magazine. Can you do this, Miss
Ellsworth? Will you do it? And if you will, how long will it take, do you
think?"

Ruth Ellsworth is one of four librarians comprising the professional
staff in the reference department of the Memel Public Library. The library
serves a city of 225,000 with a large, varied, up-to-date collection of books,
periodicals and other materials. The general reference collection numbers
over 5,000 volumes in all fields, since there are no subject departments at
Memel, and is especially strong in current bibliographies and indexes. The
reference department houses an extensive file of current pamphlet material,
including many government documents. Photocopying equipment is available.

The Memel Public Library provides no special services to the handicapped or homebound. There are no written policies concerning reference
service, although as a matter of unwritten policy it is understood that answers will not be provided for medical or legal reference questions or those
relating to school assignments. The amount of time to be devoted to an
individual inquiry is left to the discretion of the individual staff member.

• • • • •

If you were Miss Ellsworth, how would you respond to Mr. Brewer's
request for assistance? Should the reference department, in this particular
instance, undertake to locate and assemble source materials on which an

article could be based? What specific steps would be involved in this, and what specific reference sources should be consulted? What information is available on the subject of the use of federal funds for antithetical purposes that could serve as the basis for an article for a popular magazine?

14.
Suspected Plagiarism
. . . .

Metro University is one of the fifteen largest privately supported institutions of higher education in the United States, with an enrollment in excess of 20,000 students in undergraduate and graduate daytime, evening and extension courses. It is located in one of the great urban manufacturing and financial centers of the country, and most of its students come from the middle and lower class urban neighborhoods that surround it. Although it is often sneered at in academic circles for its reputedly low standards, the very size of the university and the range and magnitude of its offerings is impressive. In addition to undergraduate majors and graduate degrees in the arts and sciences, and the usual professional disciplines, Metro also offers degree programs in such diverse fields as police science, applied aviation and mortuary science.

Metro University has grown so rapidly that its library has had great difficulty in building resources and staff quickly enough to keep up. In the past twelve years, the library has outgrown two buildings, and a third, designed to house a collection of three million volumes, is currently under construction. Meanwhile, the largest collections, numbering approximately 750,000 volumes, are located in the Arts and Social Sciences Library, which occupies most of the central administration building. Quarters are crowded, but morale is generally high among the staff, both because a spacious new building which will permit centralization of collections now scattered in more than a dozen departmental libraries is in prospect; and because the university administration has been liberal in providing funds for materials and staff.

The professional staff of the Metro University Library enjoys an especially favorable position. All members of the professional staff have full faculty status, and are compensated on an equal basis with the teaching faculty and research staff. As a result of this, and because of the strength of the union which represents both faculty and library staff, beginning professional salaries at Metro University Library average nearly $2,000 a year higher than current national norms among large academic libraries.

For the past three years, Metro University has been the scene of almost continual demonstrations and protests. The chief targets have been ROTC (which has been abolished as a consequence of bloody and violent demonstrations), on-campus recruiting by war-related industries, military research, and university admission policies with respect to members of minority groups. State and local police have been called to the campus on the average of once a month during the last two years, and on three occasions units of the National Guard have been summoned to Metro. By virtue of these events, however, many far-reaching and fundamental changes in the structure and character of the university have been accepted by the administration and faculty, including an open-enrollment policy, now in its first full year of operation, which has resulted in a freshman class that is nearly one third non-white.

Ronald Norridge has been Assistant Director for Public Services of the Arts and Social Sciences Library for the past two and one half years. Nothing in his previous experience as reference librarian at one of the Ivy League colleges had prepared him for the environment he found at Metro, but he has managed to maintain, and even improve upon, the level of service offered by the several departments of the library for which he is responsible. Norridge has a reputation as a fair-minded, hard-working and competent supervisor, who is flexible, receptive to new ideas, and willing to give members of the staff a real opportunity to participate meaningfully in the decision-making process.

Late in January, Mr. Norridge was away from the campus for approximately ten days. On the morning he returned to the library, as he passed through the reference room, he called a friendly greeting to James Crisfield, the youngest and most recently appointed member of the staff of the reference department. Norridge had learned during his two and a half years at Metro to be alert to the slightest sign of a problem, and sensing that Crisfield's response was somewhat less enthusiastic than usual, he decided to stop and chat with the young man for a moment.

"How are you Jim? How's everything?"

"Oh, O.K. Ron."

"Well, what's been happening while I've been away? Been busy in reference?"

"Yeah, sort of, I guess you might say busy. But you'll hear all about it when you get upstairs."

"That sounds kind of ominous, Jim. What's the problem?"

"Oh, you'll get it all from Martha. Yeah, Old Martha's up in your office right now, just waiting for you to get there, so she can lay the whole thing on you."

Mr. Norridge's smile faded at the tone of apparent bitterness which had been obvious in Mr. Crisfield's last remark. The younger man was clearly agitated, and Norridge assumed that he had had some sort of disagreement with Martha Dalton, the head of the reference department and Crisfield's immediate supervisor. Miss Dalton had been a member of the staff of the Metro University Library for over twenty years, and head of the reference department for the last ten of those years. Although she was an able and conscientious staff member, she was what Norridge often termed "an old-school service librarian," excessively reserved in manner, conservative and inflexible. While she was respected both by the staff and by those members of the university community who knew her, she had little or nothing, by way of creative ideas, to offer in her role as head of a major public service department. Norridge accepted her as an inheritance from the past with which he had to live, and tended to work around her whenever possible. He recalled that she had been strongly opposed to Mr. Crisfield's appointment, referring to him as "a dirty hippie" because he wore a beard, had long hair and did not wear conventional clothing. In vain, Norridge had attempted to point out to her that Crisfield was an unusually bright, promising young man who could be expected to be particularly effective in establishing rapport with students and younger members of the faculty.

"So you had some kind of run in with Martha Dalton while I was gone? I'd like to hear your version of it, Jim."

"Look, Ron, I just don't want to talk about it right now, O.K.? I mean, it's all part of something a lot bigger about this whole scene. You're a good guy and you've always been straight with me, but I just can't take it with old Martha, and that's it. I mean, if we're not here to help the students—if we're just here to be flunkies for the faculty and reinforce the whole institutional racism bit—then, forget it man!"

"I'd still like to hear what happened—your version, I mean."

"Wait till you hear old Martha's version. She's really uptight. You know how you're always telling us that we have to exercise professional judgment at the reference desk and in handling our assignments?"

"Yes."

"Well, I guess you could call this a difference of professional judgment. But it's really much more than that, in my opinion. It's a whole question of what this library and this university are all about, I think. Look, let me ask you this: what is the library's policy on reference service to the faculty?"

"Reference service to the faculty? I don't think we have a policy as such—I mean any kind of written policy statement."

"What would you say our policy is, then?"

"Well, in general, it seems to me that the job of the reference staff is to provide any type of reference or bibliographical assistance that is requested by individual members of the faculty, within the limits of our resources—resources of staff time, materials, and so on."

"In other words, the reference staff are faculty flunkies?"

"No, I wouldn't put it that way. A reference librarian has a special kind of expertise—bibliographic expertise—which he makes available in support of the teaching and research programs of the university."

"What about the students? What is our responsibility to them?"

"Pretty much the same, I'd say—to provide specialized expert assistance on request, along with our instructional responsibility to try to make them knowledgeable about how to use the library. But what exactly is your point, and how does all this relate to your problem with Martha?"

"Look, Ron, I said I'd rather not talk about it, and here I am ready to dump the whole mess on you before you've even gotten in the office door. But, you'll hear it anyway, so it might as well be from me first. Do you know Fairfield in English?"

"Ralph Fairfield?"

"Ralph Proctor Fairfield, Ph.D., V.I.P., etc., etc."

"Sure, I know Ralph. He's not exactly the world's most lovable person."

"As a matter of fact, he's an arrogant anglophile and an intellectual snob. He treats the people in this department, from Martha on down, like we were his personal servants. We wind up doing half his work for him, and he acts like he's doing us one hell of a favor by letting us do it. But that's not really what got to me. What got to me was what he wanted us to do. You know, he's one of the most overt racists on campus."

"I know he was very strongly opposed to open enrollment and the Higher Horizons admissions programs."

"And to the Black Studies program. I think he introduced a motion to have the faculty senate censure the administration on that one."

"Maybe so, Jim, but that doesn't make him a 'racist.' Not in my book."

"From what I've heard from the students, it's in the classroom that he really comes through clearly. He just about comes right out and tells the blacks that they're inferior, that they don't belong at Metro, and that he's there to flunk them out. And the irony of it, or the tragedy, depending on your point of view, is that they've got him teaching a section of Special English for freshmen. Anyway, he came down to the department last Tuesday and told Martha he was sure he'd caught a black student plagiarizing on his term paper. He claims this kid lifted an analysis of a character in *Bleak House* right out of some book or journal, changed a few words, and submitted it as his own work. Of course, he's all set to go to the dean and the administrative board and get the kid tossed out. But the problem is, he doesn't know what source the student has plagiarized from. And, he's got seventy-five papers or something to read and grade by Friday, before the end of the exam period. So, he wants us to locate the source."

"So?"

"So, Martha falls all over herself as usual, yessing him to death, tells him to leave the paper, and tells the whole staff to drop everything else and start searching the critical literature on Dickens to find the source. And, as she will no doubt tell you, I refused."

"You refused? Why?"

"My God, Ron, if you don't see why—if you really don't see why— then there's just no point at all."

"Jim, humor a tired middle-aged man. Tell me why."

"Ron, there isn't anything funny about this at all. I'm dead serious. But I'll tell you the reasons, not necessarily in order of importance. One, I happen to think that my job here is to help students, not to be a faculty flunky. Two, six people have worked on this for four days, and still haven't located the source. I think that staff time should have been devoted to activities that would be of some constructive value to students. Three, Fairfield represents everything that's wrong and irrelevant about this university —about the whole elitist bit in American higher education. He doesn't want to teach black students anything—he doesn't want change—he just wants to defend the status quo and the academic establishment by flunking some poor black kid out of the school. O.K., he can do that—for the moment, he has the power to do that, but I can't and won't be a party to it. If this is what the library is for, then I think the students who want to burn it are right!"

"Jim, I'm sorry this happened, and that it's gotten you this agitated."

"Ron, my question is, whose interests are we here to serve? Are we here to work with and for the students, or does 'reference librarian' just equal 'faculty flunky' at Metro? I'd like to know your answer to that."

"I don't think our choices are quite that simple, nor do I guess that this is the best time for rational discussion of the questions you're raising."

"I don't think there's anything to discuss, Ron. If I don't have the right, as a member of the professional staff, to refuse an assignment that is not only distasteful, but diametrically opposed to what I consider the purposes of a university library, then I've got to either try to change the system or get out, one or the other."

As Jim Crisfield had predicted, Miss Dalton was indeed waiting for Mr. Norridge when he reached his office. She confirmed that Mr. Crisfield had refused to help locate the source of the suspected plagiarism. Beyond that, she reported, he had tried to persuade other members of the reference staff to refuse to take part in the search as well, and suggested that they conceal the source from which the student paper had been plagiarized, if one of them should locate it. She told Mr. Norridge that Mr. Crisfield had discussed the matter widely with students, and that another member of the reference staff had told her that Crisfield had written letters reporting the incident both to the president of the campus chapter of AAUP and to the Black Student Organization. Beyond this, she advised Mr. Norridge that Mr. Crisfield had presented the matter to the grievance committee of the faculty-staff union, and that she, the director of libraries, Mr. Norridge and Mr. Crisfield were scheduled to meet with the grievance committee in a formal negotiating session three days hence. Finally, she told Mr. Norridge that she considered Mr. Crisfield's conduct in this matter insubordinate and unprofessional, in that he had both refused to accept a legitimate work assignment and violated the confidence of Professor Fairfield's reference inquiry. In Mr. Norridge's absence, she had immediately brought the matter to the attention of the director of libraries and urged that Mr. Crisfield be summarily dismissed from the staff. In response to a question from Mr. Norridge, she said that in her opinion the student paper in question was clearly plagiarized from some published critical source.

Shortly after Miss Dalton left his office, Mr. Norridge had a telephone call from the director of libraries, who asked him to meet with him at the noon hour to prepare a response to the grievance committee and to determine what action, if any, should be taken with respect to the continued employment of Mr. Crisfield.

• • • • •

Assuming that the circumstances relating to this incident are essentially as Mr. Crisfield and Miss Dalton have described them, how would you evaluate the arguments on either side if you were in Mr. Norridge's position? Do you feel that Mr. Crisfield had, or should have had, the right to refuse an assignment which was distasteful to him in principle? How would you expect the Black Student Organization to react to Mr. Crisfield's complaint? How would the student body in general react? The AAUP? The faculty? The faculty-staff grievance committee? The director of libraries? The library staff?

If you were Mr. Norridge, would you support Miss Dalton's recommendation that Mr. Crisfield be dismissed from the staff? If not, would you ask him to accept a transfer to another department?

15.
A Marketing Survey

· · · · · · · · · · · · · · · · ·

As James Hampton, Chief Librarian of the Tarim Public Library, entered the public reading room, he was surprised and pleased to recognize the familiar figure of Paul Uvalde waiting at the charging section of the circulation desk.

"Hey, Paul! What brings you to the library?"

"Oh, just thought I'd come down and see if you're giving the taxpayers an honest day's work for that big fat paycheck you collect every week."

"Listen, friend, as I've told you many times, if I were after a fat paycheck, I'd be in the used car business like you. What are you up to, anyway? Checking the guides to luxury hotels for your next Caribbean cruise, or what?"

"Don't I wish it. Not this year, Jim. With Dad just out of the hospital, we're sticking close to home this winter."

"How is your dad? I saw him just the other day."

"Oh, he's feeling pretty good, but he's supposed to be taking it easy. To him, that means getting down to the garage at 7:30 every morning, six days a week. You can't talk to him about taking it easy. In fact, talking to him about anything can drive you up the wall sometimes. Man, I . . . say, Jim, I just thought of something. Maybe you can help me out. Got a minute?"

"Sure, Paul. Something to do with the library?"

"Well, I was hoping I could find some information about advertising. Does the library, by any chance, subscribe to any advertising magazines?"

"No, Paul, we don't. We only take about a hundred current maga-

zines, and they're all pretty much the general ones. We try to stick to
things that are indexed in the *Reader's Guide.*"

"I thought I might be able to find what I'm looking for in the *Wall
Street Journal,* but I checked through some of the back issues over there
without any luck. Is there any kind of index to that?"

"Paul, I think there is an index to the *Wall Street Journal,* but I
know we don't have it. It's too expensive and we don't have enough of a
backfile yet to make it worthwhile. We only started getting the *Journal*
about a year ago. But we do have the indexes to the *New York Times* for
the last five years, as well as the *Times* on microfilm for the same period.
Would that help you at all?"

"Microfilm? No, I don't think so. How about the Hooper surveys,
have you by any chance got any of them?"

"If I knew what they were, I'd be able to answer your question."

"Well, I've never seen them, but they're supposed to be marketing
surveys on the effectiveness of certain forms of advertising."

"I doubt very much that we'd have them. I can't recall ordering or
seeing anything like that in the two years I've been here. And I handle all
the book orders, except for children's books. No, I'm really quite sure we
don't, if it's recent. Is it?"

"I haven't seen it, but I guess it must be fairly recent. I thought
maybe the *Journal* might have something about it. I'd like to get some
information on it, if there's anything available at all. Or get a look at the
Hooper survey itself, if I could."

"I wish we could help, Paul. Maybe if I knew a little more specifically what you're after?"

"Actually, it's a business matter, Jim. I don't like to say anything
about it."

"I don't want to pry into your business, Paul, believe me. But I might
be able to come up with what you want, if I had a little better idea of just
what it is you're after. See what I mean?"

"I don't quite see how. I mean, if you're pretty sure you haven't got
the Hooper surveys, then you just don't have them, that's all. After all,
this is a small town library, and you can't expect to find specialized stuff
here. I know that. And I'm not even sure these Hooper things are available
anyway. They may just be for advertising and marketing people, you know?"

"Could be. But let me check in the business department of the Trent
Public when I'm over there on Friday. I go over once a month for the

regional advisory council meeting, and if I can manage to get there early enough, I'll see what I can find out. Do you want the Hooper survey, if I can get it on interlibrary loan for you?"

"Yeah, sure! But I don't want to put you to all that trouble. Besides, by Friday, Dad may be onto something else and have forgotten all about it."

"Oh, it's your dad who wants it. Well, in that case, I'll make it a point to see if I can get it for him. Goodness knows he's helped me out lots of times."

"No, Jim, that's not it. Look, I don't like to tell my business all over town, but if you're going to go to all that trouble, you'd better know the whole story, not just half of it. See, Dad and I had a little disagreement about our advertising policy. You know we sponsor the basketball telecasts —the home games and the regionals?"

"Sure. I've seen them on TV."

"Well, the basketball games were my idea. Dad's never thought much of it, because of the cost, you know. Anyway, Kilgore from KXBX has been trying to convince us to switch our advertising to radio. You get a lot more exposure for the money, but I favor the TV. Who listens to radio anymore? Well today, Kilgore cornered Dad down at the Elks at lunch and told him about this Hooper survey which supposedly proves that if people see a commercial on television once, all you have to do is repeat the sound-track on radio and they'll mentally see the television picture. See, it's an argument for cutting back on television advertising, which is pretty expensive, and investing that money in radio advertising. Anyway, all afternoon Dad's been talking 'Hooper,' 'Hooper,' 'Hooper,' and telling me we ought to drop the TV advertising for radio. So, to keep peace, I told him I'd look into the Hooper survey, and see what it's all about."

"Now I understand. Let me see if I can get hold of the survey, or something about it for you."

"Thanks Jim. If you can, I'd really appreciate it."

The Tarim Public Library serves a small city of 15,000 in a rural area of the midwest. The library is reasonably well supported for a community in this size range, but the book collection of under 30,000 volumes provides little specialized material. After his conversation with Mr. Uvalde, Mr. Hampton consulted the card catalog under the heading "marketing" and found two titles listed with publication dates of 1964 and 1951. The index to the older work contained no reference to "Hooper" and the more recent title was not on the shelves. Mr. Hampton decided it was unlikely he could locate any information about the Hooper surveys in the Tarim Public Library's general reference collection, which numbered about 400 titles, was limited to the most basic and frequently used items, and included little or nothing in the field of business beyond *The Economic Almanac* and a regional directory of manufacturers. He decided instead to try to obtain either a copy of the survey or information about it in the course of a forthcoming visit to the public library in Trent, the nearest large city to Tarim.

The following Friday morning, Mr. Hampton arrived at the Trent Public Library approximately forty-five minutes before the scheduled starting time of the meeting which he had come to attend. Trent is a city of 95,000 people. The Trent Public Library, with a collection of over 200,000 volumes, is by far the strongest in that section of the state, although in terms of national standards for public libraries in communities this size it would have to be described as mediocre, with respect to the quality of its resources. Mr. Hampton went directly to the business reference department of the Trent Library, where he was disappointed to find that the business librarian, who was the individual most familiar with the library's holdings in that field, had left two days earlier for a month's vacation. The assistant on duty was unable to provide any information about the Hooper survey beyond the fact that there was no listing under "Hooper" either in the department's card catalog or in the general catalog of the library.

• • • • •

If you were Mr. Hampton, how would you go about locating either a copy of the survey sought by Mr. Uvalde or information about it? What information about the survey can be obtained through either general reference sources or specialized sources that might reasonably be expected to be available in either the Tarim or Trent public libraries? How would you evaluate Mr. Hampton's handling of the reference interview with Mr. Uvalde and his subsequent efforts to locate the desired information? What alternative ways of providing the information, if any, might have been explored?

16.
An Epigram

· · · · · · · · · ·

"Miss Staunton, are you awfully busy right now?"

"Not if there's something I can do to help you. Come on into the office. Let me see, you're . . . ?"

"Eileen Marengo. I'm in Mrs. Clinton's English class. You came to our class last week."

"Of course, the 10th grade English class—the college preparatory group. You're new at North this year then?"

"Yes. As a matter of fact, I guess I'm even newer than the other sophomores, because we just moved here this year. We lived in Panama before."

"Is that so?"

"Yes. My father's in the army, so we move around a lot. North sure is a great place. I've never seen anything like this before. And the library is just fantastic. At the school where I went last year, all we had was a little room with a few scraggly books."

"Well, I'm glad you like North, Eileen. I hope you'll have a good year, and it's nice to have a chance to get acquainted with you. But you wanted help with something, didn't you?"

"Actually, Miss Staunton, I don't know if I ought to be bothering you with this, because it isn't really anything for school. Is it O.K. to ask about something that's not for school?"

"Try me, and I'll tell you if it's not O.K."

"I'm really sorry to bother you, but it just makes me so darn mad! See, last night at home we were watching this movie on TV called *The Man Who Never Was*. Have you seen it?"

"No, I don't think so, though the title sounds familiar."

"Well, actually it's sort of a neat movie. But the thing is, at the beginning there's a poem. Just part of a poem. And my father thought that poem was really great. So he wanted to know where the whole poem was from. And I said it was pretty easy to find things like that, if you knew how to use the reference books in the library. You know, like you were telling us in English?"

"That's right. You can find almost anything, if you know how."

"Well, I guess I just don't know how. I used that little book you gave us about how to use the library, and I've looked in the *Index to Poetry*, but it just isn't there. Can you tell me where else to look?"

"You've looked in Granger's *Index to Poetry?*"

"Yes, that's the one."

"What's the title of the poem, do you know?"

"No, I don't. And I don't know who wrote it. But I've got the quote from it written down. Should I look in a quotation book?"

"Let me see the quote first. Then we'll decide."

Eileen produced a sheet of lined yellow paper, on which the following lines were written:

Last Night I dreamed a deadly dream—
Beyond the Irish sky
I saw a dead man win a fight
And I think that dead man was I.

Miss Staunton studied the text for a moment:

"You know, Eileen, I think I know where that's from."

"Miss Staunton, you're something else. Do you really?"

"I'm not absolutely sure, but I think that's from Yeats' poem about the Irish Airman. Come on, let's take a look."

Miss Staunton led the way to the 800 section of the shelves, and quickly located a copy of the *Collected Poems* of William Butler Yeats. Upon turning to the text of "An Irish Airman Foresees His Death," however, both she and Eileen were disappointed to find that the poem did not contain the lines they were seeking. Miss Staunton checked the first line index in the *Collected Poems* without success. Next, she and Eileen checked the indexes in *Granger* and in Stevenson's *Home Book of Verse*, but to no avail. At that point, Miss Staunton paused for a moment to assess the situation:

"Well, Eileen, it looks as if your poem isn't going to be as easy to find as I'd thought at first. Do you have time to do some more searching?"

"Yes, this is my free period."

"Then I'd suggest checking the first line indexes in the backs of the anthologies of poetry—English and Irish, if we have any Irish."

Miss Staunton and Eileen Marengo devoted the next twenty minutes to searching through two dozen or more general anthologies of English and American poetry, but "Last Night I dreamed a deadly dream" did not appear in the first line indexes of any of them. At length, Miss Staunton said: "That's the last of the anthologies that's on the shelf at the moment, and your poem doesn't seem to be in any of them. Do you want to do some more looking? If so, I'd suggest you stop by at the main public library on your way home from school today, and check through the anthologies of Irish and English poetry there."

North High School is located in a medium-sized city on the eastern seaboard, and has an enrollment of approximately 2,400 students in grades ten through twelve. The North High School library is well established, with a strong collection of over 20,000 volumes which is kept current by regular and meticulous weeding. The reference collection contains nearly 1,000 titles, including all of the reference books recommended in the *Senior High School Library Catalog*, plus many titles selected from *Choice* and other current lists for secondary school and college libraries. The staff includes two librarians in addition to Miss Staunton, and three full-time media aides. Non-print materials are integrated into the collections, with the exception of films which are handled through a separate office.

• • • • •

What is the source of the quotation for which Eileen Marengo is searching? What is the most efficient means of locating the desired text?

How would you evaluate Miss Staunton's handling of the reference interview and subsequent search? Would you have handled it differently? Would your final suggestion to Eileen Marengo have been different from Miss Staunton's?"

17.
A Busy Afternoon

· · · · · · · · · · · · ·

"Julia, does the library have anything at all on Bach? There's nothing listed in the catalog."

Julia Amory, reference librarian at Tiber State College, looked up to find Edith Wellston, a member of the faculty in the physics department, standing in front of the reference desk.

"I'm afraid we don't have much on music, Mrs. Wellston, but if there's a particular book on Bach you're looking for, we might be able to get it on interlibrary loan."

"There certainly isn't much on music, or on many other things, for that matter. Really, this library is pathetic!"

"Well, as you know, it's a problem of space and money. Until we get the new building, we just don't have space to shelve anything that isn't directly needed for instructional purposes. But if you'll tell me what book you want, I will try to see if we can locate a copy for you."

"What I need is information, rather than a book. And to get information, there's no substitute for a good library. That's what I really miss out here, being so far away from good libraries."

"Yes, it's true there's not much in Tiber or the immediate area except for the college library, with all its limitations. What is it exactly that you're looking for? We might have something on it."

"I wanted information on the Bach *B-minor Mass*. I've checked *Groves*, but it doesn't give me what I'm looking for."

"What is it exactly that you're looking for?"

"Something about the *Mass* itself. My husband and I drove over to Irrawaddy on Sunday, for the choral society concert. Were you there, by any chance?"

"Unfortunately, I'm not much of a concert-goer, and I'm afraid I don't know very much about choral music."

"Well, it was quite a good concert. But the reason I stopped by the library this afternoon was to see if I could locate an explanation of one section of the program notes. Let me show you here what I'm after. It's this section I've underlined."

Mrs. Wellston pointed to the following marked section of text in her concert program:

"The *Mass in B-Minor* left Bach's hand without title or indication of the use he wished made of it. It is clear that it could not have been intended for the Roman liturgy. There is not merely the evidence of Bach's division of the composition into four parts as contrasted with the Roman five *(Kyrie, Gloria, Credo, Sanctus* and *Agnus Dei)* but the separation of the *Sanctus* from the *Osanna* and *Benedictus* (a separation which may be historically justified but which is liturgically impossible). This marks the *Mass in B-Minor* as a profoundly Lutheran work, quite distinct from Masses by Catholic composers."

She continued:

"We understood the business about the separation into four parts instead of five in Bach, but what we don't understand at all is the parenthetical comment. We don't understand why the separation of the *Sanctus* from the *Osanna* is either 'historically justified' or 'liturgically impossible.' I thought it was just ignorance on my part, but the friends who were with us at the concert, and who are Roman Catholics, don't understand what it means either. I was just curious, that's all. But *Groves* sheds no light on it. And I suppose you haven't anything else?"

"Would you like me to check and see if I can find anything on it?"

"There's nothing in the card catalog under 'Bach,' of that I can assure you, because I've looked myself."

"Well, I might be able to find something in some other source."

"I'd be very grateful if you could. I'll be in class for the next hour, but I'll drop by again before I leave for home."

Mrs. Wellston left the reference room, again promising to return in slightly more than an hour's time. Miss Amory confirmed that the card catalog contained no entry under "Bach" as subject. She had just returned to the reference desk to consider alternate ways of locating information on the *B-Minor Mass* when the telephone rang.

"Reference room, Miss Amory."

"Julia, this is Louise in the dean's office. Dean Kalispell wondered if you would be willing to look something up in the dictionary for him?"

"Sure."

"He wants to know what you call the space that's formed by the intersection of two circles. Do you know what I mean?"

"I'm not sure I do, Louise."

"Well, you have a circle, right? And you draw another circle beside it, so that the two circles partially overlap. Then you have one section that is common to both circles, do you follow me?"

"Yes, I do."

"What the dean wants to know is, what is the special name for the overlapping section that is common to both circles?"

"Oh, sure, it's like a Venn diagram."

"Is that what it's called, a Venn diagram?"

"No, Louise, that's what Venn diagrams look like. I remember them from a course in computers I took in library school. I don't know what the scientific name for the space within the two circles is called. Hold on, I'll try to check it in a math dictionary."

Miss Amory walked to the reference shelves, and returned to the telephone a few moments later to continue the conversation:

"Louise, I can't find it right off hand. We do have a math dictionary, but it seems to have disappeared at the moment. Probably some student walked off with it. Does the dean need this right away?"

"I'm typing a manuscript for him that he wants to proofread this afternoon, because he's leaving in the morning for a week's trip to the west coast. And I'm stuck without that name. I can't go on with the typing."

"Can't you just leave a space and keep typing?"

"I can't. It comes in the middle of a line."

"Well, take a coffee break. I'll try to call you back on it as soon as I have the answer."

Miss Amory turned from the telephone to find two students waiting at the reference desk.

"Are you waiting for me? Can I help you with something?"

"I need to find this." The student held up a mimeographed sheet which read as follows:

"On page 205 of your edition of *A Portrait of the Artist as A Young Man,* Joyce refers to a song by Ben Jonson of which he quotes the first line: 'I was not wearier where I lay.' Find the source Joyce is quoting."

The student continued:

"I've checked Jonson's *Collected Poems* and I can't find any poem beginning with that line."

"Does the edition of Jonson you're using have a first-line index?"

"Yes, in the back. That's where I checked."

"I see. And is this young lady looking for the same thing?"

The second student responded:

"No, I'm from the Student Arts Festival Committee, and I'm trying to find something I can quote from reviews of the film *Black Orpheus.* We're showing *Black Orpheus* during the festival, and I want some quotes for a flyer and a press release. Quotes from the critics. Is there any kind of an index to film reviews?"

"Not a separately published index to film reviews, no. Or, if there is one, we don't have it in the library."

"Do you know any way I could find reviews? I know you have back files of magazines and things, but I don't know exactly when the film came out or was reviewed first. And the other thing I wanted to ask you was, do you know how much you're allowed to quote from a magazine? I mean, because of copyright?"

Tiber State College is located in a rural area, approximately sixty miles from the nearest city of any substantial size. The college has an enrollment of 2,700 students, including approximately 900 graduate students in education at the masters level. About half of the undergraduates are majoring in elementary or secondary education, the remainder being distributed among the liberal arts disciplines, the sciences, or enrolled in the department of business administration. The college has, for the past ten years, been in the process of effecting a gradual curricular shift from teacher training to the liberal arts and sciences at the undergraduate level. Most of the available liberal arts curricular options have come into existence during this decade.

In bringing about this basic change in the nature of the undergraduate curriculum, members of the faculty of Tiber State College have been handicapped by the limitations of the library, which long ago outgrew its present quarters. Limitations of space and funds have compelled the library, for the

last six years, to restrict current acquisitions to titles directly related to the
instructional program. The book collection numbers only slightly more than
90,000 volumes, of which nearly 10,000 have been placed in storage for
lack of shelf space, until a new library building is constructed three years
hence. The chief areas of strength in the general book collection are education and related fields, and historical material concerning the region in
which the college is located. The periodical collection is also relatively good,
having been strengthened in recent years by the systematic purchase, under
a special grant, of twenty-five year back files on microfilm of titles covered
in the *Reader's Guide to Periodical Literature* and the *Social Science and
Humanities Index*. Back files of professional periodicals in the field of education are also extensive. The reference collection numbers approximately
500 titles, which have been chosen with particular emphasis on bibliographies
and indexes to facilitate identification of materials for interlibrary loan, and
which reflect the major areas of instructional emphasis at the college, with
the exception of the laboratory sciences. The library staff includes four
professionals, with Miss Amory solely responsible for the reference desk,
which is not staffed during those hours when she is not on duty.

• • • • •

If you were Miss Amory, how would you deal at this point with the
reference questions raised in this case study? What priorities would you
establish among them? Why? Which sources would you use, or suggest be
used, to locate the information sought by each of the four inquirers? How
much searching, in each individual instance, would you expect or have
time to do yourself? Is it possible to locate answers, within the time available, to each of the several questions raised in the case through materials
that are known to be available, or might reasonably be assumed to be available, at the Tiber State College Library? What are the answers to the questions raised by the two students, Dean Kalispell's secretary and Mrs. Wellston, respectively? Will additional information, which should have been
obtained through the reference interview, be needed to locate satisfactory
answers to any of these questions?

18.
Accusations
from the 'Right'

· · · · · · · · · · · ·

"Helen, this is Roger Spooner. Have you seen this week's *Crier?*"

"Yes, I've seen it. How are you Roger?"

"Damned angry, that's how I am. Have you seen the editorial page?"

"Yes. It's right here on the desk in front of me. I suppose it's another volley from Chief Rhinelander."

"Yes. Rhinelander, and that idiot Cudahy at the *Crier.*"

"Well, Roger, they're both ignorant men, so what can you expect? Don't let it get your blood pressure up."

"Get my blood pressure up! That's exactly what it's done. I'll not be called a 'Communist' by some illiterate Fascist done up in a storm trooper's uniform. Nor do I imagine my fellow trustees will enjoy it much either. But the main thing, Helen, is—you mustn't be upset by all of this. You must keep calm, at all costs."

"Roger, you're a sweet man to worry about my feelings, but I assure you, they're completely intact. We've been this route before with the Chief, and we've always come out fine, because you and the other trustees have always supported your own book selection policy and me as your executive officer. Besides, Roger, I'm the town librarian and an employee of the board, which means at least I get paid for taking this kind of gaff. You poor people don't even get a check on the first of the month for being called 'fellow-travellers.' "

"I suppose this all stems from the World Peace Seminar last month? The Chief never did get over our allowing that in the library auditorium."

"Yes, he wasn't too enthusiastic about that was he? Of course, he's still stewing over the Earth Day film program."

"Against that too, I suppose?"

"According to Herman, our janitor, the Chief spoke over at the veterans' hall, and, as I understand it, pronounced Earth Day and all kindred activities a 'Communist plot to weaken our moral fiber.' But, tell me, how's the board taking the *Crier*'s editorial?"

"If Edith Rawlins is any example, not well at all. It's going to come up at the board meeting tomorrow night. And I understand there will be reporters present, both from the *Crier* and from the *Telegram.*"

"The *Telegram!* Wow! We've made the big city papers at last."

"It's not funny, Helen. Edith is getting weary. And some of the other board members may be getting weary too. We stand to lose everything you and I have gained for the library and the town over the last three years at that meeting tomorrow night. Edith's making noises about 'reviewing' our book selection policy. And all over a piece of utter nonsense that some irresponsible idiot chooses to print in a small town paper. I just wish I knew who wrote that blasted 'Communist Rules' thing. Personally, I suspect Rhinelander wrote it himself. It's the same sort of unintelligible trash he's always spouting."

"I agree it does have the ring of Rhinelander about it. But the word from the 'boys,' according to Herman, is that it's cribbed from a veterans' organization magazine. Do you suppose I ought to try to find out the actual source?"

"Helen, that's just what I called you about. I think it's imperative that we know the original source, and have the full text before us at tomorrow night's meeting. The board had better know just exactly what we're up against. Would Herman know?"

"Roger, Herman couldn't produce a bibliographic citation to save his life. And if I asked him, he'd run right over to the 'hall' and ask the 'boys.' Or over to the station and ask the Chief. I'll have to play reference librarian and see what I can do."

"I think it's quite important, Helen."

"O.K. Roger. You're the chairman of the board, and if you say it's important, it's important. I'll have it for you."

A few minutes later, her telephone conversation completed, Helen Keyser, Director of the Nile Memorial Library, sat contemplating the front page of the *Valley Crier*, the weekly newspaper for the town of VN_____, in which the Nile Library is located. The editorial to which the chairman of the library board had referred in his conversation with her was the latest episode in a campaign of criticism of the library which had been carried on intermittently since shortly after her arrival in VN____ by a small, but vocal and influential segment of the community which objected to her liberal policies in book selection and library programming. In her efforts to inform the community about what were, in her view, vital contemporary issues, and to raise the level of the book collection above light fiction and home handicrafts, Miss Keyser had early run afoul of the local chief of police, who considered himself personally responsible for the moral wellbeing of the town and all its citizens. When his friendly visits and polite 'advice' were ignored, he had turned to public criticism and political pressure, of which the following front-page editorial was the most recent example:

From the editor's desk:

THE LONG ARM OF COINCIDENCE?

Publication of the following was requested by a member of the Police Department. We urge all citizens to consider it thoughtfully.

"In May of 1919, at Dusseldorf, Germany, the Allied Forces obtained a copy of some of the 'Communist Rules for Revolution.' A half-century later, the Reds still follow the 'Rules.' As you read the list stop after each item and think about the *present day situation where you live* and around our nation. We quote from the Red Rules.

Corrupt the young—get them away from religion. Get them interested in sex. Make them superficial; destroy their ruggedness.

Get people's mind off their government by focusing their attention on sexy books and plays and other trivial matters.

Divide the people into hostile groups by constantly harping on controversial matters of no importance.

Destroy the people's faith in their national leaders by holding the latter up to contempt and ridicule.

By specious argument cause the breakdown of the old moral virtues— honesty, sobriety, continence, faith in the pledged word and ruggedness."

Quite a list, isn't it? Now stop and think how many of these rules are being carried out in our town and in our nation today. I don't see how any thinking American can truthfully say that the Communists do not have any part in the chaos that is upsetting our nation. Or is it just one big coincidence? I doubt it! Take, for example, what's been happening lately to our public library. *Let's listen to those who know before it's too late!*

The Nile Memorial Library serves a community of 30,000 in a semi-rural section of the northeast. The nearest large city is almost an hour's drive away over country roads, and its public library has no significant resources for reference work or research. The Nile Library has a collection of approximately 50,000 volumes, many of which are trivial or out-of-date titles. Since her appointment as the first professionally trained director of the library three years ago, Miss Keyser has made a systematic effort to strengthen the book collection by purchasing many of the less expensive titles which appear in the latest edition of the American Library Association's *Reference Books for Small and Medium-sized Public Libraries.* Beyond these, there is little by way of current reference material available locally. The card catalog of the library contains no entry under the title "Communist Rules for Revolution," and a search under appropriate subject headings has made it clear that the text of the source document for this week's *Valley Crier* editorial is not to be found as a monograph in the collection.

• • • • •

What is the source document on which the *Valley Crier* editorial is based? How does the original text compare with the *Valley Crier*'s version? What can be determined with respect to the authenticity of the original text? How can the original source document be located most expeditiously by Miss Keyser, working within the limitations of sources that are known to be or might reasonably be assumed to be available to her? Of what value to the Board of Trustees of the Nile Memorial Library will location of the original source document on which the newspaper editorial is based be?

19.
The Pass System
. . . .

At the Kagera Public Library, which serves a large eastern city, the monthly
meeting of department heads, presided over by the library director, Miss
Grinnell, provides opportunity for the exchange of a variety of kinds of
information and ideas. At the August meeting, those present, in addition
to Miss Grinnell, included the assistant director, Mr. Newton; the head of
adult services, Mr. Zeigler; the head of circulation, Mrs. Bettendorf; the
head of branch and extension services, Mr. Chanute; the head of reference
services, Miss Hoisington; the head of children's services, Miss Albia; and
the head of audio-visual services, Mrs. Fredonia. The head of the technical
processes department and the art and music librarian, who customarily
attend department heads' meetings, were both on vacation and so not present
when the discussion recorded in this case study took place.

After Miss Grinnell had disposed of several items of routine business
and made a few announcements, she turned to what she had mentally
designated as the "major agenda item" for the morning:

"I don't know if all of you have yet had an opportunity to get to
know Elaine Albia, who has been with us just a few weeks, but I want to
begin discussion of a recommendation that she has made by saying I think
she's done a superb job in getting to know the system here in a very short
time and in evaluating the strengths and weaknesses of her own department.
Now she has a proposal which would affect several other departments, and
I've explained to her that under our own little version of participatory
democracy here at Kagera, such matters are thrashed out at these monthly
meetings so that everybody concerned has an opportunity to express himself before any final decision is made. I have decided, after a very short

acquaintance, that Elaine is quite capable of speaking for herself, so I propose to let her do just that."

MISS ALBIA: "Well I'm very glad to have this chance to thank all of you for being so helpful to me in getting familiar with both the library and the community. With your help I've been able to see and learn a great deal in the two months I've been here. I think you have a lot to be proud of in this library, and that Miss Hobart did an outstanding job in building up the children's collection in the last years before she retired.

"I know all of you admired Miss Hobart, and although, coming from another part of the country, I knew her only by reputation, it's clear to me that she ran an excellent department in many respects. I do think you'll probably find my approach and ideas about children's service a little different from hers, and I'll welcome your reactions to them. I know too that you've been concerned, as evidently was Miss Hobart before her retirement, about the decline in circulation in the children's department, particularly here at the main library. Although this kind of circulation loss seems to be just about universal, as school libraries are meeting more and more of the needs of elementary school children, I think we have to find ways—imaginative new ways—to counteract this trend. A lot of my ideas along this line have to do with increased use of media in the children's department and a great deal more by way of programing for children than we've been able to do in the past. I don't want to take your time to go into these things in detail now, but what I did want to bring up at this meeting is one specific problem. Or, rather, one specific recommendation.

"I want to abolish all the regulations that restrict the free movement of children through the library. I want the library to adopt a policy whereby children are free to go anywhere in the library, into any area that is open to the public, and use any library materials they need, without having to ask permission from anybody. That's the policy I'd like to see adopted before the new school year begins next month and that's what I've asked Miss Grinnell to do."

MR. ZEIGLER: "Perhaps I'm missing the point, but I don't find anything very earthshaking in that. Children are perfectly free to use the adult collections now. They just get a pass from the children's librarian on duty."

MISS HOISINGTON: "That is true for the reference department, too, but I believe, Louis, that Miss Albia is proposing to do away with passes. At least that was the impression I got in my conversation with her last week. And, before we get into any discussion of this, I would like to say again to Miss Albia, and to Miss Grinnell, whom I haven't had an opportunity to speak with about this, that the reference department would be completely and unalterably opposed to doing away with passes. Passes are the only control we have. Without them, it would be chaos. We simply couldn't handle it."

MR. ZEIGLER: "Oh, I quite agree, Ann. It would be bedlam. There has to be a control. Otherwise it's pandemonium. Not that it isn't on some days already, once the school year starts."

MR. NEWTON: "I can see it all now. The little beggars racing through the stacks, dumping the trays in the card catalog, ripping pages out of the encyclopedias. Disaster!"

MISS GRINNELL: "Now you can all see why Walter is a bachelor. He obviously hates children. But I think we owe it to Elaine Albia to at least listen to her reasons before we jump all over her idea."

MISS ALBIA: "Very briefly, my reasons are these. First, the child below high school age, through grade eight, is being treated as a second-class citizen by this library, because he is restricted to the children's room without a permission slip from the librarian. It's discrimination against a particular group because of age, and I think that's wrong, on the face of it. That idea may amuse some of you, but I can tell you that children, especially older children in the upper grades, just hate it. They hate these restrictions. They hate having to ask permission to get into the reference room and into the general book collection. It creates in their minds a negative image of the whole library as a place that keeps them down because they are kids. As a consequence, they use the library as little as possible during high school, and not at all, in many instances, once they become adults. You've lost them forever because of the negative image you've created by these restrictions.

"Second, the division between child and adult is a totally arbitrary one—the completion of the eighth grade. It ignores the very well known, established fact that individual children mature at different rates. There are children in Kagera, just as there are everywhere, who are reading adult material in the fourth and fifth grades, let alone the seventh and eighth. And there are teenagers and adults who would be far better served by material that we have in the children's room. The barrier works both ways, but it's the child who has to get permission, not the other way around. But my point is that to create such a great barrier between children and adults in the library does everybody a disservice in the long run.

"Thirdly, the present system is totally unrealistic in terms of what's happening in schools these days. I already know enough from talking with the people on the staff to be certain that this children's collection, like any children's collection, is simply not adequate to meet the informational and school needs of kids in the upper elementary grades. They need to use the reference room, the general periodical collection, and they need to use microfilm. Every year, more and more is expected of them by the schools. The school libraries recognize this, and the public library has to recognize it too, by opening up the total resources of the library to every child, not on an individual basis, not as some kind of special favor, but as a regular, routine thing that you don't have to ask permission for.

"Fourthly, and then I'll shut up and let you people talk, the making out of permission slips is an utter waste of staff time. By and large the children know precisely what they need and where to find it. They're not naive when it comes to knowing how to use the card catalog or how to find something in a periodical index. They learn these things in elementary school today, and if you aren't aware of that, you just don't know what's happening in schools. Fifth and sixth graders know more about how to use the library and how to locate information than most adults do. All they need is a little initial orientation."

MISS HOISINGTON: "As Miss Albia knows, I have heard these arguments now for the second time and they simply ignore the reality of how we must operate in this library. It is clear to me that if we were to abolish the system of permission slips, as I sincerely hope we will not, it is the reference department that would be chiefly affected. There might be some minor disciplinary problems for the guards and for the adult department, but the reference department would bear the brunt of it."

Miss Hoisington's observation was received with general murmurs and nods of agreement from the other department heads present, including Miss Albia. Miss Hoisington continued:

"That being the case, I restate as strongly as I can my complete opposition to any proposal to eliminate permission slips. The fact is that the reference department simply cannot handle the present work load. First, because we do not have the space. There are, at maximum, seventy-five seats in the reference room. During the school year, especially during vacation periods, every seat is taken and people are sitting on the floor. If elementary school children are allowed into the reference room without restriction, they will force high school and college students and adults out.

"Second, we cannot do it because we do not have the staff. My staff of seven people handled over 80,000 reference questions last year that we were able to record. Beyond this, we are constantly having to run to the stacks for books or back issues of periodicals—hundreds, on busy days. We have the microfilm readers to take care of. The staff of the reference department just cannot manage any more. If we have the elementary school children turned loose on us, we had better plan either to double the staff of the department or replace the people we have, because the present staff would resign *en masse*.

"As for the younger children, we are just not equipped to deal with their needs. My people do not want to work with children. If they did, they would have become children's librarians, not reference librarians. We're not trained for that work, or interested in it, as I believe most, if not all, of the people on Miss Albia's own staff in the children's department would agree. They don't want this change either, from what I've heard."

MISS ALBIA: "I know I promised to give you people an opportunity to speak, but I would like to comment on one or two points that Miss Hoisington just made. For one thing, Miss Hoisington has just given the perfect illustration of my point about children being treated as second-class citizens by the library. When space and staff are limited in the reference room, it's the children who are automatically denied the service. Why can't it just be on a first come, first served basis, with children having the same opportunity for reference service as anyone else? And as far as people in the reference department learning how to work with younger children, that's just a matter of a little training and experience, which I'd be only too happy to help out with."

MR. ZEIGLER: "But children aren't denied reference service. You have a reference collection in the children's room, don't you?"

MISS ALBIA: "Yes, but it doesn't approach adequacy for children beyond grade three. You can't meet their needs for information with a handful of juvenile encyclopedias and a couple of dozen periodicals. And it would be absurd and wasteful to duplicate materials that are right next door in the reference room."

MR. NEWTON: "How about the staff in the children's department, Miss Albia? Have you discussed doing away with permission slips with them?"

MISS ALBIA: "Yes, I have. If you took a poll, you'd find right at this moment that most of them would probably vote against it. I'm afraid it's because, almost without exception, the staff of my department is limited to people who've been trained in this library and have never worked anywhere else. They've been indoctrinated in a kind of maternalism in working with children which I don't share or agree with."

MISS HOISINGTON: "But surely permission slips aren't unique to this library. All libraries use this system. It's standard procedure."

MISS GRINNELL: "Could I ask, Miss Albia, if permission slips were used at the Niemen Library?"

MISS ALBIA: "I agree that it is a common system, but that doesn't make it right. We did use slips at Niemen, though I tried for years to get them to abolish the system. Unfortunately, I was not the head of the children's department there, and I was never able to convince my boss that the system was outmoded."

MR. CHANUTE: "I wonder if you are suggesting a change in the branches as well? Would you want to do away with permission slips there too? As I think you know, with one very small exception, every one of our branches has a totally separate children's room."

MISS ALBIA: "Yes, I'd like to open up the whole system. I just find the pass system hateful, whether it's at the central library or in a branch."

MR. CHANUTE: "That would present quite a few problems."

MR. NEWTON: "Ann, you said earlier that if we did make this change, you thought we'd have to double the staff in the reference department. Was that rhetorical, or were you serious?"

MISS HOISINGTON: "Completely serious, Walter. My little staff can't begin to handle the present workload. There must be over 10,000 children of elementary school age in this city, almost every one with a library card."

MR. NEWTON: "When you talk about doubling the staff, you mean the professional staff?"

MISS HOISINGTON: "I certainly do. There's no point in hiring nonprofessionals for the reference department, as I've told you many times before. We have no time in reference to run a training program."

MR. NEWTON: "I don't suppose you'd foresee our being able to reduce the staff in the children's department if we abolished the passes?"

MISS ALBIA: "No, I don't. I really don't believe this would represent any kind of major shift in workload. What it would do is eliminate the waste of staff time that goes into writing out permission slips, and change the negative image the children have of the library."

MR. ZEIGLER: "But what about the negative image on the part of adults who come in and find children running through every part of the building? I think we need permission slips for control of the building, and to make certain that youngsters who can get what they need in the children's room don't become a burden for the reference staff."

MRS. BETTENDORF: "As I've listened to this discussion, I've been wondering more and more if we aren't confusing building logistics with service?"

MISS GRINNELL: "Possibly so, but I think we've given as much time to discussing Miss Albia's proposal as we can this morning. Perhaps we could continue with this at our next meeting, and meanwhile try to consider the whole question as rationally and objectively as possible in our own minds."

MISS HOISINGTON: "Forgive me, Miss Grinnell and all of you, but at the risk of sounding disagreeable again, as I'm afraid I have all morning, I have to say that I don't think anything would be gained by further discussion. These theoretical discussions are fine, and a great many things sound lovely in theory, but they just won't work for good, sound, practical reasons. I do not dislike children. I think they are lovely, in their place. But their place is not in the reference room. This is my firm view, and no amount of discussion will convince me otherwise. If we did not have the permission slip system for control, I could not remain here at Kagera, and I think I can safely speak for the other people in the department as well. I don't feel that anything will be gained from further discussion. A decision will simply have to be made."

• • • • •

How would you evaluate the arguments presented by Miss Albia in favor of abolition of the permission slip system at the Kagera Public Library and those presented by Miss Hoisington and other members of the staff in favor of its retention? What principles of reference service are involved here? What would your own position on the question be?

Is the use of permission slips common in public libraries? If so what are the reasons for it? Does this constitute a form of discrimination against children, as Miss Albia suggests?

If you were Miss Grinnell, how would you respond to Miss Hoisington's final statement? By whom, and in what manner, should Miss Albia's recommendation that permission slips be abolished be brought to a point of decision?

20

A High School Drop-Out

· · · · · · · · · · · · · · · · · · · ·

The Roger Thames Library serves a city of nearly one million in the north-central United States. Although the city suffers from most of the problems that generally beset contemporary urban America—a vanishing middle-class population, a growing multi-racial ghetto, a diminishing tax base, expanding welfare rolls, deteriorating schools, a rise in crime and racial tension—the Thames Library has been spared the direct effects of these to a greater extent than most other major metropolitan public libraries. Thames has long been among the leading libraries of the nation, and is considered a model of public library practice. A series of able administrators, each of whom has enjoyed unusually long tenure, sound management of massive endowment funds, and excellent recruiting and staff development programs, combined with effective public relations on a city-wide basis, have kept Thames in a flourishing condition during a decade when other urban public libraries have been fighting for their very existence.

The Thames Library was one of the first public libraries to organize central collections and public service departments along subject divisional lines. The nine major public service departments in the main library are Language and Literature, Music, Art, History and Travel, Science and Technology, Business and Economics, Philosophy and Religion, Social Science and Documents, and General Reference. The central building also houses a small Popular Library, as well as central technical services and administrative offices. The subject departments are staffed by individuals who are specially qualified by experience and/or academic training to develop and interpret the collections in appropriate fields of knowledge.

The General Reference Department contains those bibliographical tools, periodicals, and monographic materials which do not fall within a single subject area, as well as small collections in a few isolated fields, such as sports and games, that cannot readily be related to any of the subject departments. General Reference also functions as a central referral point for inquiries coming into the library which those manning the switchboard or the information desk in the lobby cannot direct at once to one of the subject departments. The union card catalog is adjacent to the department, and one of the functions of the "G.R." staff is to assist the public in its use.

General Reference is a busy department, handling, each year, a huge number of quick reference and directional questions. Much of the routine work at both the telephone and reference desks is done by a corps of twelve library technicians, several of whom are college graduates and all of whom have been carefully trained by the professional staff. The central library is open to the public seven days a week for a total of eighty-five hours, and at least one librarian is on duty in General Reference at all times.

Friday evenings tend to be rather quiet in the department, and for that reason only one librarian is scheduled to be on duty between 6 p.m. and the 10 p.m. closing hour. One Friday evening in mid-August, Gerald Canton, who had joined the staff of the Thames Library just six weeks earlier in his first professional position after graduation from library school, was sitting at the supervisor's desk in the General Reference Department office, a glassed-in space immediately behind the public reference desk. He noticed that Ben Madera, the library technician on duty at the desk, was engaged in animated conversation with a young black man who appeared to be in his late teens. The conversation continued for some time before Mr. Madera turned and came into the office.

"Mr. Canton, I've got a beautiful reference question for you! This one will really drive you nuts! Do you see that kid out at the desk? Well, he's never been in the library before in his life. He wandered into Popular Reading and told them his problem, and they sent him up here. If anybody can help him, it will have to be you, because I haven't got any idea where to send him or what to give him to look at. But first, let me just brief you to save time, because he's obviously scared to death of the library and everybody who works here, and it will take you half an hour to drag the problem out of him.

"To begin with, this kid is a high school drop-out who's taking a night course over at Boys Vocational, trying to get his equivalency certificate. He works six days a week in a garage, and goes to school nights to pick up the academic subjects he flunked before he dropped out of regular school. He's taking English this summer, which he's got to pass, or no equivalency certificate. His story is that his English teacher has it in for all black kids, but especially for him. Anyway, they got into some kind of a hassle—he and this English teacher—and the English teacher says he's going to flunk him unless he hands in a thousand-word research paper next Monday night. The kid says nobody else in the class has to write the research paper, just him. Evidently, from what I gather, it's some kind of punishment assignment, because the others in the class have never had to write anything longer than 300-word papers, and haven't had to do anything that required research or using the library. The school library at Boys Vocational isn't much to start with, but anyway, it's closed for the summer, so the teacher told this guy to come here to do his research. I really feel sorry for the kid. Passing this course is tremendously important to him, and, in my opinion, he's totally unprepared to begin to do anything like what he's being asked to do. He doesn't even know what a reference book is! And this is the assignment he's been given to complete this weekend: Prepare a documented research paper of not less than 1,000 words, including not less than ten library references, in support of, or in opposition to, the following statement by the noted Orientalist Wm. Theodore De Bary: 'China's long history, like that of other major Asian civilizations, can be characterized as introverted and intensive in its development, as compared to that of the West which has been more extroverted and extensive. In general, Western civilizations have tended to look outward on the world and Asian civilizations to look inward.'

"Mr. Canton, isn't that an unbelievable assignment to give an eighteen-year-old high school drop-out? That teacher has certainly got it in for this kid, handing him an assignment like this. Anyway, he's got to get this done tonight and, he's got just about ninety minutes before the library closes. He wasted a half hour down in Popular Reading before he got the courage to ask anybody to help him. I know you're not supposed to do students' assignments or research for them, but if there ever was an exception to that good old 'G.R.' policy of long standing, this has got to be it. Anyway, I'll send him into the office. He's all yours!"

• • • • •

If you were Mr. Canton and, like him, had no special knowledge of

Oriental cultures or history, what specific suggestions and/or assistance would you give to the student described in the case? How would you advise him to go about completing his assignment in the context of the Thames Library within the time available to him? To what extent would you apply or modify the policy of the General Reference Department with respect to reference service to students which is reproduced in the Appendix?

APPENDIX

Excerpt from the *Staff Manual* of the General Reference Department, Roger Thames Library:

STUDENTS

The recommended policy in serving students is based on the belief that members of the reference staff have a clear responsibility to encourage them to learn the elements of self-service and guide them in the search for material.

Students should be given directions for finding books, periodicals and the like, rather than having these found for them.

The reference assistant should recommend procedures for finding material on a subject rather than assembling exact data for the student. Students should be referred to the card catalog, periodical indexes, encyclopedias or bibliographies and shown how to use them if necessary.

Many school assignments present considerable difficulty because of the lack of available material or because a thorough search would take an unjustifiable amount of time. Adult patrons, who have no other library service available to them, should never be kept waiting while students are given assistance.

21.
An Awkward Question

· · · · · · · · · · · · · · · · · ·

"Miss Harahan, I'm sorry to interrupt, but I urgently need to speak with you."

"Mrs. Lemont, I'm afraid that I'm busy just at the moment, as you can see. These gentlemen are from the redevelopment authority, and we are going over the plans for the new South Branch."

"I know that you're busy, Miss Harahan, and believe me, I would not interrupt if it were not an emergency."

Barbara Harahan, Director of the Rhone Public Library, hastily excused herself and went to the open door of her office where Edith Lemont, chief reference librarian, stood, looking extremely distraught.

"Miss Harahan, we are having trouble at the reference desk, and I simply must ask you to come down and handle it. Please! Will you come at once?"

"Of course, Mrs. Lemont, if it's that urgent. But what on earth is the trouble? Is it a fight, or something? If so, let's call the police."

"Miss Harahan, please! Come with me, and let me show you."

Mrs. Lemont led the way rapidly to a balcony overlooking the reference room. To Miss Harahan, the scene below appeared to be typical of a normal, moderately busy spring afternoon. The long tables in the reference room were, as usual, occupied by a few adults and many high school and junior high school students. She did notice that the room was surprisingly silent, considering the number of people in it. Because their voices would carry from the balcony down into the room below, Miss Harahan spoke softly.

"Mrs. Lemont, I'm completely mystified. What is the emergency? I don't see a thing."

"Look again, Miss Harahan. Do you see that person standing by the reference desk?"

"You mean the young man there near the atlas case?"

"Yes, he's the one. I've simply told him that he will have to talk with you."

"Why? What is the problem?"

"The problem is—I don't know what sort of dirty business he's up to, but I'll have nothing to do with him, or his kind. Miss Harahan, I just don't know what to say to him or what to do."

"Mrs. Lemont, you're obviously very upset, and you're not making sense. Besides, we're attracting an audience. Let's step back here into the alcove, where the people down below can't see us."

"That's what's so embarrassing. Everybody in the reference room overheard him."

"Who? The young man at the desk? Well, what does he want?"

"It's not what he wants—it's what he is."

"For heaven's sake, Mrs. Lemont, what is he?"

"I think he's one of those 'queer people.' "

" 'Queer?' You mean, like 'mentally ill?' "

"No, Miss Harahan. I mean 'queer.' I mean (her voice lowered to a whisper) 'feminine.' He came up to the desk, and I thought there was something odd about him. Just the way he walked. And then, he says that he's looking up some information for a friend. And what he wants is to find out which states will allow two men to get married legally. And he wants to know which churches will allow it."

"Which states allow homosexual marriage? I don't imagine any do, do they?"

"I'm certain I don't know, and I don't want to find out. It just makes my flesh crawl. And everybody in the room heard him. See how they're staring at him."

"Yes, they are. Tell me, did he actually identify himself as a homosexual?"

"No, he didn't use that particular term. He calls it 'homophile.' That's the name he used."

"Homophile. Well, I think it means about the same thing. But, anyway, what did you tell him?"

"Well for a minute or two, I just was speechless. Couldn't say a word. Then, finally, I told him I was sure we didn't have anything in the reference room on that. But he insists we do. Says his friend told him he could find out about those things at the library."

"So, what did you do then?"

"Well, I didn't know what to do. He just wouldn't go away! Finally, I told him I'd speak to the head librarian about it."

"That's when you came up to my office?"

"Of course. Frankly, I hoped he'd be gone by the time I got back with you. I should think he'd be embarrassed."

"Yes, so would I. But the thing is, Mrs. Lemont, you seem to be the one who's embarrassed by all this. Now, pull yourself together. I know it's awkward, but surely the young man isn't doing you or anybody else any real harm."

"Will you come down and speak to him? Get rid of him?"

"If you want to get rid of him, I'd suggest you help him find the answers to his questions. Mrs. Lemont, you're a trained, experienced reference librarian. You've been on the staff of this library for nearly fifteen years, and you know more about reference work and the reference collection than anyone else here, including me. If anybody can help that poor young man find what he's looking for, you can. Now, I'm very sympathetic with the way you feel, and I know it's shocking and difficult for you, but you're just going to have to go back downstairs and help him find what he's looking for."

A look of utter horror came over Mrs. Lemont's face at Miss Harahan's final words.

"Miss Harahan, I won't do it! You can fire me right here on the spot, if you want to, but I absolutely refuse to go near that . . . that queer again."

The Rhone Public Library serves a city of nearly 90,000 through a central library and five branches. The library is well supported and ably administered, and the collections in the central library, numbering close to 200,000 volumes, are unusually strong in reference materials, journals, and substantial monographic works. The general reference collection has been selected by using the Enoch Pratt Free Library's *Reference Books* as a buying guide.

Edith Lemont was appointed head of the reference department four years ago, one year after Miss Harahan became Director of the Rhone Public Library. Mrs. Lemont is nearly fifty years old, a graduate of an accredited library school, with more than twenty years experience in reference work at Rhone and elsewhere. She is generally recognized by all members of the staff as an efficient, dedicated and capable person. There are no other professionals on duty in the reference room at the time the incident described in this case study occurs.

• • • • •

If you were Miss Harahan, what would you say or do at this point? Would you insist that Mrs. Lemont help the young man to locate the information he is seeking? Or would you handle the problem in some other way?

Assuming that Mrs. Lemont, Miss Harahan, or some other member of the staff will undertake to locate the information being sought, what sources should be consulted? In which states, if any, are legal marriages between members of the same sex possible at the present time? Which religious denominations, if any, or individual churches, will perform a homosexual marriage ceremony?

22.
Third Party Candidates

· · · · · · · · · · · · · · · · · ·

Loire College for Women is located in a sparsely settled, rural area of the northeastern United States. With an enrollment of 1,800 undergraduate women, and a faculty of 250, Loire has, during the more than seventy years of its existence, enjoyed an excellent reputation, being particularly well known for its strong departments of music and theatre arts. Tuition and residence charges are high at Loire, and throughout its history it has been almost exclusively a school for the daughters of the affluent.

The Loire College Library is housed in a handsome building which provides more than adequate space for its collection of approximately 175,000 volumes, along with seating and study areas for about one fourth of the student body. The reserve book room is, by far, the busiest place in the library, and only during the examination period do the reading rooms ever approach a state that could be termed "crowded." Because demands on the reference collection by students are few, only one member of the staff, Eloise Marmet, is assigned to reference service. Miss Marmet, who has been reference librarian at Loire College for the past twelve years, is on duty and available each weekday when college is in session from 9 a.m. to 4:30 p.m. (except during the noon hour). The reference collection, which contains nearly 2,000 volumes, has been carefully selected from *Winchell, Choice,* and other standard book selection aids for academic libraries. Miss Marmet dutifully orders new and recommended titles each year from an ample budget, and her only complaint is that many of the reference sources seem to be little used in relation to their high cost.

Since the daily burdens of reference work are not extremely heavy at Loire, Miss Marmet devotes a good deal of time to revising the work of student assistants who file in the public catalog, checking in current issues of periodicals and new government documents which are not of sufficient long-term value to be cataloged and added to the permanent collection, and performing similar tasks. She is a pleasant, friendly, cheerful woman who is well adapted to the pace of professional life at Loire. One of her great pleasures is assisting members of the faculty with their bibliographical and research problems. In the case of students, however, Miss Marmet feels that her function should be one of instruction in the use of the library and reference materials, since it is her opinion that the faculty prefer students to "do their own work." There is no formal instruction in the use of the library at Loire, except for a thirty-minute freshman orientation tour of the building conducted in the early fall by students on the Junior Welcome Committee.

In recent years, some younger members of the faculty at Loire have begun making efforts to break down prevailing patterns of traditional text-book instruction, and provide juniors and seniors in at least some departments with modest opportunities for independent study. Especially noteworthy in this respect has been the political science department, where two young instructors have been conducting an honors seminar for juniors and seniors. Miss Marmet has become aware of this during the last two years, because of the increased number of requests for such items as the constitutions of the new nations of Africa, which are not to be found in the collections of the Loire College Library.

Friday afternoons are customarily a quiet time in the reference room. One Friday afternoon, just after lunch, a young woman, obviously a student, approached Miss Marmet:

"Excuse me, can you help me? I'm looking for the statistics."

"The best place for that is right over here in the reference room. Why don't you come along with me, and on the way you can tell me a little more exactly what you're looking for. What sort of statistics are you after?"

"Election statistics."

"You mean voting—election results?"

"Yes, that's right."

"Is this for a course? Something for a class assignment?"

"Yes, it is. Are all the statistics in one place?"

"Oh no! Statistics are all by subject. For example, statistics on elections would be in the political science section. That's in the 300's. But maybe you'd better tell me a little more precisely what you're looking for."

"O.K. See, this is for my independent study, which I'm doing with Mrs.

Omak. It's the seminar in political group theory and behavior. My paper is on the Wallace movement. Mrs. Omak got me started by saying in class that a third party candidate couldn't win the American presidency today."

"You don't agree with that?"

"Well, see, I'm from the south, and I think people up here don't really understand how strong the third party movement is down there. That's really what my paper is about. But Mrs. Omak doesn't agree with me. She says she wants to see some 'documentation,' what she called 'statistical evidence.' "

"You've already submitted the paper?"

"Oh, yeah. It was due two weeks ago. But Mrs. Omak handed it back to me to rewrite, so I've got to add some statistics and hand it in again next Monday."

"That doesn't give you much time."

"Oh, I can get it done over the weekend all right. I just need to get some statistics that show how third party candidates have done in the past —regionally I mean."

"Just in presidential elections, is that it?"

"Well, in national elections—president or congress. The whole point is that it's national."

"But it's regional statistics that you need?"

"Yes, state by state and city by city. Urban vs. rural, for example, that kind of thing. Do you know where I can find that?"

"Yes, as a matter of fact, I do. There's a set called *America Votes* that has a very detailed breakdown of national election statistics. I can't recall the call number off hand, but we don't keep our set on reference. It's in the circulating collection. You go to the card catalog and look it up under the title. It's the most detailed thing available on election statistics. I think there's one volume for every two years."

The student dutifully wandered off in the direction of the card catalog. About fifteen minutes later, she returned, empty-handed, to the reference desk:

"Couldn't you find *America Votes?*"

"It's out. I asked at the desk."

"The whole set is out?"

"That's what the girl at the desk told me. Can I get the statistics or the book any place else?"

"This afternoon, you mean?"

"Yes, I've got to get the statistics today."

"Well, if you have a car, I suggest that you drive over to the public library in Euphrates. Have you ever been to that library?"

"A couple of times when I needed stuff I couldn't get here. They have a pretty good collection."

"Yes, it's a good deal larger collection than ours, and only about a twenty-minute drive. And, I *think*—I'm almost positive—that they have a complete set of *America Votes* in their reference collection. Of course you wouldn't be able to take it out, but you could copy out the statistics you need. Would you want to do that?"

"I guess I could. I'd planned to spend most of the afternoon in the library anyway. Thanks very much."

The student disappeared, and Miss Marmet returned to her work. A few minutes later, however, she was surprised to find the same student again standing in front of the reference desk. Miss Marmet's voice began to betray a slight suggestion of impatience and irritation.

"I see you decided not to go to the Euphrates Library."

"They haven't got *America Votes* either. It was stolen."

"How do you know?"

"I thought I'd better call before I went all the way over there. The lady there told me on the phone that their set's been stolen. They're replacing it. She said it wouldn't do me any good anyway, because it only goes back to 1954. See, I need to go back right to the first contested presidential election in 1796."

"Well, let me think what else we might have that would give you presidential election statistics in that kind of detail."

Miss Marmet turned to the shelves behind the reference desk, and took down her personal copy of the eighth edition of Winchell's *Guide to Reference Books*. Consulting the index under the heading "election statistics," she was referred to items CI61–CI66. Here, in addition to *America Votes*, she found six other titles listed. Of these, only Robinson's *The Presidential Vote* was listed in the Loire catalog, and the student, when sent to search the shelves for it, promptly reported that it too was charged out. Probably, Miss Marmet reflected, by the same person who had borrowed the library's set of *America Votes*.

"While you were checking the shelves, I've been reading the annotations in this section of the *Guide*. It looks to me as if this book, *A Statistical History of the American Presidential Elections*, ought to have just what you're looking for. We don't have it, but you might be able to get that at Euphrates."

"I'd better call them, though, before I go all the way over."

The student headed off in the direction of the pay telephones, while Miss Marmet wondered how she would ever cope with the reference work if Loire College were to adopt independent study for the entire student body. A few moments later, the student appeared again.

"Well, I talked to the lady at Euphrates, in the reference department there. They've got Petersen's *Statistical History* . . . all right. The only thing is, she can't guarantee that it's in. All she can tell me is that it's listed in their card catalog."

"She couldn't check the shelves for you?"

"No, she says they don't do that for people over the phone. Besides, I guess they're pretty busy. The only thing is, if I drive over there and they haven't got it, I just won't have time to come back here again. What do you think I ought to do?"

Glancing at her watch as she thought about how to reply to this last question, Miss Marmet realized that the student had already been in the Loire College Library for over an hour, and was still without the statistical data she needed.

• • • • •

What alternatives, if any, other than going to the Euphrates Public Library in search of Petersen's book, could be suggested to or explored with the student at this point? Evaluate the alternatives in comparison with a trip to the neighboring library. How much additional time, if any, would you recommend Miss Marmet devote to this particular student? Evaluate the manner in which the student's inquiry has been handled thus far, both in terms of applicable principles of reference service in college libraries generally, and in terms of Miss Marmet's policy of "encouraging students to do their own work."

How can the specific statistical information sought by the student be located most efficiently in this situation?

23.
Knitting in Braille
. . . .

Patricia Lamont is the newest staff member of the reference department of the St. Lawrence Public Library, which serves an eastern seaboard city of 275,000 people. Miss Lamont joined the staff at St. Lawrence just three weeks before the events described in this case study, immediately after graduating from library school. Rated by her library school instructors as one of their most promising graduates, Miss Lamont received offers of employment from a number of major public libraries around the country, but chose St. Lawrence partly because of its east coast location and partly because it offered an opportunity to work under Gwendolyn Sterling.

Gwendolyn Sterling, head of the reference department at the St. Lawrence Public Library, is one of the best known people in the reference field. She is a prolific author and reviewer, an officer and committee chairman of several important professional groups, and a leading spokeswoman for public library reference service, both nationally and internationally. Her article "Ideals in Municipal Reference Service" is required reading in nearly every American library school. She has received numerous professional honors and awards over the course of her thirty-year career, all of which has been spent at the St. Lawrence Public Library. To Patricia Lamont, the opportunity to work under the direction of Miss Sterling represented the chance of a lifetime for a young person intending to make a career in the reference field.

The reference collection at St. Lawrence is an unusually strong one which would do credit to a library serving a community three times the size of St. Lawrence. Coverage of the reference literature in business and technology is particularly extensive, as a consequence of Miss Sterling's special interest over the years in providing good reference and information service to local business and industry. For the first two weeks, Miss Sterling assigned her first assistant, Mrs. Rupert, to orient Miss Lamont to the department, and Miss Lamont "shadowed" Mrs. Rupert during the hours when the latter was assigned to a public service desk. This week, Miss Lamont has been assigned to work independently at the catalog information desk, one of the three points of public service for which the reference department has responsibility. Miss Sterling and Mrs. Rupert have told her that the catalog information desk is the easiest initial assignment for a neophyte, and that after a few weeks there she will also have scheduled assignments at the general reference and business reference desks, which require considerably more skill and familiarity with the department. Miss Lamont has also been assigned responsibility for weeding and adding to the file of mounted pictures maintained by the reference department and culled chiefly from duplicate periodicals which are to be discarded from the collections. This, along with reviewing and selecting new reference books in the fields of music and art, is to be her permanent staff assignment during hours when she is not scheduled at a public service desk.

Work at the catalog information desk consists chiefly of assisting library patrons in locating items in the card catalog and answering telephone questions about the library's holdings. For the most part, Miss Lamont has had no difficulty in handling this desk assignment, since virtually all of the questions are easily answered by reference to the card catalog. Today, however, she has found it necessary to seek help and has entered the departmental office to find Miss Sterling busy at the typewriter which stands beside her desk.

"Miss Sterling, could I interrupt you for a minute?"

"Certainly, Miss Lamont. Just off the desk, are you?"

"Yes, Miss Sanger relieved me at eleven. But a question came in this morning that I wasn't able to answer, and I need some suggestions on how to track the information down. I hate to bother you with it, though."

"That's quite all right. That's what I'm here for—to help you younger people. Now, what's your question?"

"Frankly, Miss Sterling, I think I probably should know how to go about finding this, but I don't, at least not right offhand. A woman called Catalog Information this morning looking for knitting instruction in Braille. It seems she has an elderly friend who's just gone blind and is very depressed and discouraged. Anyway, the elderly friend has always liked to knit, and this woman—her name is Mrs. Killingly—thinks it would cheer up her friend if she found out she still could knit, and also help inspire the friend to learn Braille, which she's evidently refusing to do. Anyway, she wanted to know if we had anything available in the collection or if we knew where instructions for knitting in Braille could be gotten. I quickly checked the catalog under 'knitting' but couldn't find a thing, so I told her I'd get the answer and call her back later today. Can you suggest where I should look, or do you happen to know the answer?"

"Well, I don't mean to criticize, Miss Lamont. You are new at St. Lawrence, and it does take a while to learn the ropes, but I think you should have transferred that question immediately to G.R., where a more experienced person would have handled it."

"Yes, I realize that normally a question like that should go to General Reference. But this woman had already told her story in considerable detail to three different people in the library. She was finally referred to to G.R., but I guess the switchboard made a mistake and she got Catalog Information instead. Before I could stop her, she told me the whole long story, and I just couldn't bear to make her tell it again. I don't think that's particularly good public relations, do you?"

"Well, I certainly have tried to make everybody in this department public relations conscious, and I'm glad you are. Our only reason for existing is to serve the public's need for information. But I'm afraid you've got a job on your hands because I don't know the answer to your question. Have you checked the card file of difficult questions at the G.R. desk?"

"Yes, I did remember that, Miss Sterling, and I checked it before coming in here. Nothing! And nothing in the card catalog. I guess I'll just have to get busy and start searching. Have you any suggestions?"

"I'd have to think about that a little. I think I know how I'd go about looking, though I don't know an obvious source just offhand. Besides, you'll be starting in on G.R. yourself next month. You'll be on your own then with questions much tougher than this one and with less time to answer them in, so you'd just as well get used to working on your own now."

"Say, Miss Sterling, I think I've got the answer. This state must have a state agency for work with the blind, mustn't it? Every state has, I think."

"Yes?"

"Well, that's probably the quickest and surest way to find the answer. I'll just phone them. They'll know."

"Possibly. But that is something we never do in this department."

"I'm sorry, I don't understand."

"I am saying, Miss Lamont, that we do not refer questions that come to us to outside sources. We answer them ourselves. That is why the city pays our salaries, and why we have spent tens of thousands of dollars to develop the kind of reference collection we have here. Your job is to search out the answer to your patron's question. If you cannot locate the answer before you are scheduled to go back on the desk this afternoon, you simply turn it over to Mrs. Rupert and she will assign it to another member of the staff. Either the question will be answered by the staff of this department or we will determine that it is unanswerable and so advise the patron. That is the procedure around here, and I'm a little surprised you haven't gotten that far yet in your study of the department manual."

"I see. You mean that you never call an outside source or refer the patron to one?"

"Not if we can possibly locate the answer in any other way, and then, only under the most exceptional circumstances. That, however, should it arise, would be a matter for Mrs. Rupert or myself to determine."

"You or Mrs. Rupert would decide?"

"Yes, the department head or first assistant is the person who determines that a given question cannot be answered. We know the collections best. But you seem puzzled by all of this, Miss Lamont."

"Well, to be honest with you, Miss Sterling, I'm a little embarrassed not to have caught this in the staff manual, which I really have studied, though it might not look that way right at this moment. But I'm also puzzled about this policy of not making use of outside sources of information. I hesitate to say this to you after such a short time in the department, but it seems sort of silly to me."

"Silly? If so, I could only observe that you have a great deal to learn about reference work beyond what your library school taught you, Miss Lamont. There are at least two very good reasons for this policy. The first is money. For example, the state capital is 150 miles from here. That's a long distance telephone call, and the library budget simply will not accommodate long distance calls on behalf of patrons. Nor should the patron have to pay the cost of a long distance call to get information that is available right here in a public library which she supports with her tax dollars. Which leads me to the second reason for handling reference questions here —public relations. We don't go to other people for information, Miss Lamont! They come to us for information! We are the community information center for this city! We've spent years educating people and businesses and agencies of government to that fact—to that image of the department and the library. That's why we've enjoyed the kind of budgetary support that has made the growth of this department possible. If we made it a practice to refer people outside the library for information, or did it ourselves, our image would change very quickly. Why we'd be nothing but a collection of high-priced switchboard operators, and I don't think the public would tolerate that very long. Call it a matter of pride if you wish, but as long as I am head of this department, this will be our policy. Now, I've kept you from your reference question long enough. You know, I envy you. I used to love tracking down the answers to questions like that one when I was on the reference desk."

• • • • •

From what source or sources may instructions for knitting in Braille be obtained? What alternative ways of locating this information are there? Which are the most satisfactory?

What is your reaction to the policy of the reference department at the St. Lawrence Public Library on the use of outside sources of information? Do you feel that Miss Sterling offers adequate justification for this policy? If the existence of such a policy came to your attention as director of the library, or as a member of its board of trustees, how would you respond to it?

If you were Miss Lamont, what suggestions would you have for altering this policy, if any? How would you go about effecting a change in policy, if you felt one was desirable?

The Study-In

. . . .

Arno State University is located in a large midwestern city. In recent years, Arno, as a publicly supported institution, has expanded very rapidly to meet ever-increasing demands. Enrollment has grown from 6,000 students to 16,000 during this period, and although numerically most of this growth has been at the undergraduate level, there has also been a proliferation of new graduate programs. More than a dozen new graduate and professional programs have been established at Arno in the past fifteen years. Dr. Robert Lamar, who has been Chancellor of Arno throughout this period of expansion, has taken the public position that the university "must be responsive to the educational needs of the people even though expansion and establishment of new programs require us to stretch our limited financial resources to the utmost."

There are many among the faculty, staff and student body at Arno who, privately and publicly, express the opinion that the university's limited financial resources have already been stretched beyond the breaking point by Dr. Lamar's expansionist policies, and that the quality of instruction leaves much to be desired. Although the state legislature has been rather easily persuaded to authorize bond issues for construction of classroom and dormitory facilities, the university community has suffered badly from inadequate laboratories and a library building that is pitifully small and overcrowded. Even more serious has been a glaring inadequacy in library materials and services. The library's operating budget represents only two and one half percent of the total educational and general budget of the university, and consequently both the collections and staff are far below accepted minimum standards.

Arno University has been the scene of a number of militant demonstrations over the past three or four years, focusing on the peace movement and the educational aspirations of minority groups. On three occasions during the past year, police have entered the campus. The most recent occasion of police action was a demonstration by black students, one consequence of which was a commitment on the part of the university to divert a substantial portion of its operating budget to the expansion of educational opportunities for minority group students. Laudable as this decision was, it has resulted in a significant reduction in funds available to support other areas of the university community. The library, already operating on an inadequate budget, has been particularly hard hit by this most recent adjustment in university fiscal priorities.

During the past few months, the university library has been the focus of a rising chorus of student and faculty complaint. Clyde Muscatine, Director of Libraries at Arno, has been characterized in the student press as "ineffectual," "unresponsive to student needs," and "a willing front man for the university administration." The truth is that Muscatine has, for years, been caught in the middle between the legitimate demands of students and faculty for expanded library resources and services and the unwillingness of the university administration to give proper priority to library needs. He has pressed the administration as vigorously as he knows how to provide needed funds, but at the same time has consistently refused to be a party to the student-faculty campaign to force an increase in library appropriations.

One morning early in the spring, Marilyn Kingman, Assistant Director of Libraries for Reference Services, appeared in Mr. Muscatine's office seeking an immediate conference with him. "Marilyn," said Mr. Muscatine as he ushered her into his office, "you look upset. What's the problem this morning?" Miss Kingman responded by handing a mimeographed handbill to Muscatine. "Haven't you heard about this? These are being posted and handed out all over campus." The handbill read as follows:

!!!   LIBRARY STUDY-IN STARTS AT NOON TOMORROW   !!!

A study-in is starting at noon tomorrow in the reference room of the library to back up demands for an adequate library. We call on everyone who is sick and tired of the vacillation and petty excuses of the university and library administration to dramatize our demands for a decent library.

The Demands

1. Muscatine must go! We demand his immediate resignation as director of libraries.

2. The university must allocate a sum to library acquisitions and operation for next year that is not less than ten percent of the total university operating budget, subject to the following conditions:

(a) The additional funds must not be gained from an increase in tuition, a worsening of the student-faculty ratio, the cutting of academic programs or the cutting of faculty salaries.

(b) There must be no reduction in the special programs for Blacks and Third World.

(c) If funds must be derived from increases in state appropriations, any tax increases which result must be derived from taxes on profits and not on wages.

3. All meetings of the university cabinet must be open to any student, faculty and staff members who wish to attend, and a detailed budget must be published for next year within thirty days.

The people who have called for the study-in have done so because they believe that the present state of the library is a severe detriment to the quality of education at the university and that the proposals that have to date come from Muscatine and Lamar for improvements are inadequate and insulting.

The intent of the study-in is to liberate the library—liberate it from bad priorities, occupation by the administrative bureaucracy, and the pressures that sacrifice good education to giving people a minimally-acceptable job training. The reference room is the nerve center of the library—a nerve center that is in fact paralyzed by lack of money for books and staff. Our job is to make the nature of this paralysis clear.

If you support the action, go to the reference room as soon as you can. It would help if faculty members would cancel their classes. Bring your books so that you can do some work while you're there. We will stay until our demands are met. No time limit has been set.

Most of the library staff is with us, though they cannot support us directly for fear of reprisals by Muscatine and Lamar. They are doing their best with what they have to work with, even though they are underpaid.

Mr. Muscatine had just finished reading the handbill when he was interrupted by the intercom on his desk. He excused himself and left the office, returning almost immediately. "Well, Marilyn, that was a call from Dr. Lamar's office. I'm to meet with him and the Provost in an hour to discuss this study-in business. They've evidently just gotten wind of it."

"Clyde, what are we going to do about this? Do we close the library, or what?"

"Frankly, I don't know. But I do know that Dr. Lamar will want a recommendation from us, although he'll have to make the final decision."

"Well, he should have to. If he'd supported the library decently, we wouldn't be facing this now. And the students wouldn't be demanding your resignation."

"Maybe so. I've tried every way I know to get Lamar to give us what we need to do a decent job here. Maybe I am ineffectual, and maybe I should resign, but I'll be damned if I'll knuckle under to this kind of student pressure. And as for closing the library, I'd just hate to recommend that. In the first place, whatever the limitations, the service we are able to give is better than no library service at all. And I won't allow a tiny minority of militant students to deprive everybody else of an essential college service, even for a day."

"I'm not sure how small a minority may be involved, Clyde. That's something we won't know until tomorrow noon. And it wouldn't take very many people to pack the reference room and catalog area full enough to shut off library service."

"True. And, if we close, the students can just postpone this until we reopen. We can't stay closed forever."

"Well, if we try to stay open, what instructions do I give the reference staff?"

"How do the staff feel about this?"

"Well, there's at least one person who's delighted, but most of the rest are pretty upset and nervous. They want to know whether they should come to work tomorrow, and what to do when a great horde of students arrives to 'liberate' them. My guess is that some of my people are pretty scared about what might happen, especially if the university decides to take a hard line or call in the police."

"How do you feel about the study-in, Marilyn?"

"That's not an easy question to answer. While I hate this kind of tactic on the students' part, the fact is that the students are absolutely right on this, and you know it! And maybe taking over the reference room is the only way to get to Lamar. We've tried all the appropriate channels— or, rather, you've tried them—to get the kind of budget we need to provide decent library service. I don't know—if I were fifteen years younger, I might join them myself."

"Well, be that as it may, it doesn't help with the question of what I should recommend to Dr. Lamar. Do we close down, because of the threat of the study-in, or not? If we stay open, what instructions will you give to your staff? I'd hate to take responsibility for asking any of our people to come to work if there's any risk of violence. And judging from what happened in January at Alumni Hall, I'd say that there is that risk. Beyond that, there's the problem of protecting the card catalog and the reference collection." Mr. Muscatine paused thoughtfully for a moment. "Marilyn, it's your people who are on the firing line with this. You tell me what recommendation you think I should make to Dr. Lamar and how you would propose to handle this. I'm not trying to pass the buck, but I can tell you that I will be guided in this matter by whatever you recommend."

• • • • •

Assuming that you were in Miss Kingman's place, what recommendation would you make to Mr. Muscatine with respect to the forthcoming study-in? Should the library remain open? If so, what instructions should Miss Kingman plan to give to members of the reference staff? What contingencies might need to be anticipated in giving instructions to the staff, if the library is to remain open?

Under the circumstances described in the case, do you feel that the study-in is a justifiable course of action on the part of students? What position would you as an individual member of the professional staff of the reference department take in this matter?

25.
A Curriculum Library

. . . .

"Curriculum Library, Mr. Gallup speaking."

"Mr. Gallup, this is Edwina Rome in the superintendent's office. I wonder if you can help us? We're doing the racial census for the Department of Education. Can you tell us how you classify Cape Verde Islanders?"

"How do you mean 'classify'?"

"I mean does the Census Bureau consider them 'white' or 'non-white'? We don't know which category to put them in."

"I'm afraid I can't answer the question offhand. But I'll be glad to check the Census publications we have and see what I can find out. It's Cape Verde Islanders you're interested in?"

"Yes. If we have to classify them as 'non-white,' two of the elementary schools in Okatown become racially imbalanced. So I hope you can find something to justify our counting them as 'white.' Can you check for us?"

"Have you tried phoning the Department of Education to find out?"

"We want to find out for ourselves before we send the report in to them. There's just no sense in calling attention to the problem if it's going to turn out that we don't have a problem."

"We haven't too much by way of Census publications, Miss Rome, but I'll check here and also with the public library. How soon do you need this?"

"The report has to be in the mail today, so we really need the information within the next hour."

"O.K., I'll call you."

Raymond Gallup, librarian of the Juba Public Schools Curriculum Center Library, had just replaced the telephone on his desk when Harold

Easton, Director of Guidance at one of Juba's four academic high schools, came into the former classroom which now housed the library.

"Ray, I'm on my way to a meeting downstairs, but I stopped by to see if you could help me out."

"Sure, Harold. What do you need?"

"I've got a call coming in this afternoon from the mother of one of our kids who graduated the year before last. He gets out of the Army next month, and he's looking for a job here where he can use Vietnamese, which he can read and speak fluently. His mother has checked with the state employment office in town, and they can't suggest anything. I've got nothing suitable in my files. Have you anything that might give me a lead on what to suggest to her?"

Before Mr. Gallup had an opportunity to reply to Mr. Easton's question, the telephone rang again.

"Curriculum Library, Mr. Gallup."

"Hello Mr. Gallup. This is Jane Salisbury at the Derwent School."

"How are you, Miss Salisbury?"

"Harassed, at the moment. I'm about to face an irate parent and I need some ammunition from you. Our policy here, and it's the policy all through the system as far as I know, has always been to separate twins, not assign them to the same class. Well, we've got a mother of twins who objects to this. She claims our policy is old-fashioned and that all the so-called 'authorities' in elementary education today are against separating twins. Anyway, she'll be here in about an hour with an armful of 'authorities' and I just didn't have time to brief myself on exactly what the best current thinking is on this question. I was hoping you might have something right there that would support our policy of separating twins in school. Can you think of anything that you could come up with rather quickly?"

The Juba Public School System serves a large urban center in the northeastern United States. For decades, the Juba public schools had deteriorated under a succession of incompetent administrators and politically inept school boards, until the withdrawal of accreditation from two high schools by the regional accrediting agency led to the election of a reform slate of school board members. They forced the incumbent superintendent into early retirement and appointed a highly qualified successor to improve the quality of the system.

One of the first concerns of the new superintendent, at the time of his appointment two years ago, was the woeful state of school libraries in the system. Only two of the high schools had certified librarians, and these presided over small, unattractive collections of little-used materials, housed in inadequate, ill-furnished library spaces. The elementary and junior high schools had no libraries to speak of, except what had been provided in a few schools through the efforts of parent-teacher organizations and volunteer groups. Initial steps have been taken to improve the library situation in the Juba Public Schools. One of these steps has been a Curriculum Center Library in the school administration building. The Curriculum Center Library, now in its second year of operation, is designed to serve as a resource center for the entire school system. Mr. Gallup, the librarian, is responsible for developing and maintaining a collection of professional books and journals in the field of education and related disciplines for use by school personnel, as well as for administering an extensive library of sample textbooks and other instructional media. He serves as a consultant to supervisors and other administrative personnel in such areas as curriculum development, and acts, unofficially, as coordinator of library and media services for the school system.

During his sixteen months at Juba, Mr. Gallup has tried vigorously to promote the image of the Curriculum Center Library as a professional information center for school personnel throughout the system. Consequently, he is often asked for reference assistance by teachers, administrators and other school staff. The library collection consists of some 4,000 professional books in education and related fields, current subscriptions to nearly 500 general and professional periodicals, and extensive files of pamphlets and federal, state and municipal documents. Some general reference books, such as encyclopedias, biographical dictionaries and directories, handbooks, statistical compendia, and national and trade bibliographies are included in the collection, although the number of these is restricted because of limitations of space and funds, which have dictated that first priority be given to the development of the professional collections. Like many special librarians, to meet informational demands Mr. Gallup depends on other libraries in the area with more extensive holdings, particularly the Juba Public Library, which has a collection of nearly half a million volumes, and is located just two blocks from school department headquarters.

· · · · ·

If you were Mr. Gallup, how would you respond to the questions raised by Miss Rome, Mr. Easton and Miss Salisbury respectively? In what order would you deal with these three inquiries, what priority of importance would you assign to each of them, and how would you go about locating the information or material sought in each instance? Of the reference sources that would be needed to locate the information being sought by each inquirer, which would you expect to find in the Curriculum Center Library? What would you consider an adequate response to each inquiry? Has enough information been obtained through the reference interview to enable the librarian to make a satisfactory response in each instance? If not, what additional information is needed?

26.
A Legal Question

· · · · · · · · · · · · · ·

"Mrs. Nokomis, there was a woman in here from the neighborhood looking for you while you were out."

Valarie Nokomis, just back from a branch librarians' meeting, smiled somewhat wearily, and hung her wet raincoat in the small closet behind her desk in the narrow, crowded workroom of the Happy Acres Branch of the Vistula Public Library.

"Well, Helen, who was the woman, and what did she want?"

"Her name is Mrs. Robbins. Do you know her?"

"Not that I can remember. I don't think so. Does she use the library?"

"I'm pretty sure I've never seen her anytime I've been on the desk."

"So how do you know she's from the neighborhood?"

"Well, for one thing, she told me that she lives over on Oak. And, for another . . ."

"I know. She's black and she looks poor and tired."

"Right. But she did act like she knew you. She was kind of upset that you weren't here. Didn't want to talk to anybody else but you. Susan and I were pretty busy when she came in, so I didn't have too much time to talk to her."

"What did Mrs. Robinson want?"

"Robbins, not Robinson. Actually, she had what I guess you'd call a reference question. I told her, though, that I don't think it's the kind of question we can answer."

"Why? What was it?"

"Well, we don't answer legal questions, right?"

"Right."

"I'd say this was a legal question, and that's what I told her. It seems that she wants to find out whether or not her son is going to be drafted. He's eighteen now, and classified I-A. But, he's just finished serving forty-five days in the House of Correction and he's on a year's probation. She wants him to be drafted and go into the Army, but she's afraid the Army won't take him because of his record."

"Why doesn't she check with the draft board?"

"That's what I suggested, but nothing doing. She won't go anywhere near the draft board. She doesn't want to give them her son's name. What she said was that she didn't want to 'call attention to herself.' Those were the words she used. I think she's afraid of the draft board—afraid to go there. But that's what I suggested she do. She did go down to Legal Aid over on Claremont, but nobody there could help her. I think she sees the library as kind of a last resort."

"I wonder how she got my name?"

"I really don't know, but she just insisted that she had to see you. She wanted to wait, but I persuaded her to give me the message instead."

"Let's see, the son is eighteen and I-A, but he's served time and is out on probation now. She wants to know if he's still eligible to be drafted?"

"Right. She seemed pretty certain that the Army wouldn't want him, because of his court record, but what she really wants to know is whether there's any way she can get him into the service."

"And you told her we couldn't answer the question?"

"I told her I didn't think we could. I did check a few things in the vertical file—recruiting handbooks, and so forth. But I couldn't find anything that gave the answer to her question. She was so nice about it, though, and so terribly concerned that I couldn't just turn her away with nothing. So I said I'd turn the question over to you when you got back later in the afternoon."

"I see."

"The thing is, Mrs. Nokomis, I wasn't sure just exactly how to handle it. I didn't know where to find the answer and I also didn't know whether this is the kind of question the library should answer. Anyway, Mrs. Robbins is coming back in about half an hour. She doesn't have a telephone, so that was the only thing I could suggest."

The Happy Acres Branch of the Vistula Public Library is located in the heart of the urban ghetto. The original branch building, constructed in 1904, was burned to the ground and its contents totally destroyed two years ago. The fire was started by a Molotov cocktail thrown through the front

window. Three weeks after the fire, the branch re-opened in the tempo-
rary, storefront quarters which it still occupies. The present book collection is small, numbering about 6,000 volumes exclusive of juvenile titles,
and the hours of library service quite limited. The staff comprises the branch
librarian, Mrs. Nokomis, a professional assistant who is currently on extended sick leave and for whom no replacement has been provided, a children's librarian, and four full-time clerks. Helen Bushnell, the senior clerk,
has worked at the branch for twelve years, and, in addition to running the
circulation desk, is accustomed to handling many of the reference questions
and other requests for assistance which arise during the course of the working day. The library is used mainly by children and young people in connection with school assignments, and by a small and relatively unchanging
group of adults who visit it chiefly for recreational reading. The reference
collection is small, comprising perhaps one hundred volumes of the quick
reference variety, and chosen to meet the needs of the student clientele,
a clientele that is diminishing slowly but steadily as the neighborhood schools
develop stronger libraries.

Valarie Nokomis became branch librarian at Happy Acres two years
ago, her predecessor having requested a transfer to the central library the
day after the fire. Conscious of all the difficulties and limitations facing an
outsider attempting to work in the black community, she has, nonetheless,
made a determined effort to bring the library into the mainstream of community life by promoting its image as a community information center.
These efforts, to date, have met with little success.

• • • • •

Assuming that Miss Bushnell has exhausted all of the obvious sources
of information on the selective service system and the military available at
the Happy Acres Branch without being able to locate a definitive answer
to Mrs. Robbins' question concerning the draft status of probationers, what
further effort, if any, would you make if you were Mrs. Nokomis? Bearing
in mind that Mrs. Robbins will presumably return to the library in approximately thirty minutes time and that the branch collection is an extremely
limited one, what alternatives would be open to Mrs. Nokomis should she
undertake to answer Mrs. Robbins' question? Which of these proves most
effective in locating the desired information?

Among a handful of policy guidelines governing the conduct of reference service in the Vistula Public Library system is the following: "Considerations of professional ethics, as well as the safety and welfare of library patrons, make it inappropriate for members of the staff to undertake to provide information on medical or legal questions. Such questions should invariably be referred to the patron's physician or attorney." Do you feel, as Miss Bushnell suggests, that this policy applies to Mrs. Robbins' question? Do you feel that prohibitions of this kind, which are traditional in public libraries, are appropriate in light of such problems as the one presented in this case?

27.
An Alaskan Valley

· · · · · · · · · · · · · ·

"Good morning, Mr. Tulare. How are you?"

"Why, it's Miss Dothan. It must be five or six years since I've seen you out here at the bookmobile. How have you been?"

"Fine, thank you."

"You run the whole library now, since Miss Piggot retired, do you?"

"That's right, Mr. Tulare."

"That's a big job for a woman."

"It keeps me busy—too busy sometimes. I guess I'm a little early getting out here this morning, but we're starting a new community stop over in Twin Pines and I wanted to ride out with the bookmobile to be on hand for it. But I'm so pleased to have a chance to see you and tell you in person how grateful we are to you for letting us park the bookmobile in your gas station garage at night. I really feel that you should let us pay you something for doing it."

"Now, Miss Dothan, I won't let you say another word about that. I owe this city a lot and this is one little way I have to repay it. I know everybody gets a lot out of having the bookmobile come around. My kids always got books from it when they were in school, and the older folks get a real kick out of it."

"Yes, that's something we hope to do more of—more community stops at nursing homes and places like that. Now that the schools are getting their own libraries they don't need to depend so much on us."

"Say, Miss Dothan, seeing you here reminds me to ask. Do you ever have any books on Alaska on this wagon?"

"I've got very little idea what's on the bookmobile anymore. But tell me what book you're looking for, and if it's not in the bookmobile collection, we might have it at the main library and could send it out to you on the bookmobile."

"Well, years ago I saw this book and for the life of me I can't remember where we got it or what ever happened to it."

"Do you remember the title?"

"No, but it was about the depression."

"About the depression in Alaska?"

"Well, these are some of the facts I remember about it. The government opened a very fertile valley that went up from above Canada. For many years they had been keeping their eye on it. The loam was about four foot deep. And they could grow enormously large vegetables—big heavy things. During the depression, the government opened it up to the people for homesteads. Many people went up there. They were allowed to take very little supplies with them on any of the trains that would lead to that part of the country. When they got there, they went into the valley and the government had an official representative there who evidently allotted the land to the different people. And the government would loan them any equipment they needed for making streets or making houses or setting up their little homesteads.

"They were given credit for every little thing they did, and they paid the land off that way. They'd all help each other build. And this was a story by two school teachers, I think, who went up there and had their home there.

"Now, what happened was, someone wrote a letter home saying that they were barely existing, that it was very hard. The letter was read in Congress, and Congress immediately sent an investigating committee up there to see what was going on. Well, it turned out there were a couple of crooked agents who were treating the people poorly, so Congress cleaned that up. And to this day, the government uses the valley for growing food."

"But you don't remember the title of the book?"

"I don't remember what it was called, but it had little sketches showing how they had to put the food up at night, up high, so the animals wouldn't get it. The people who went there were called 'pioneers.' And she said that when the excursion boats came up from San Francisco, the people would all stare at these pioneers. Those are some of the little points I remember from this book."

"You said 'she.' Was the author a woman?"

"Well, there were two that wrote it. I think maybe they both were women. Two school teachers, as I remember."

"You don't remember either of their names?"

"No."

"How about the name of the valley they were writing about?"

"It was in Alaska and . . . let me think . . . it's been so many years since I read it. I think maybe it was called 'Natuska,' something like that. An Indian or Alaskan name, wouldn't it be?"

"How would you spell that?"

"Let's see. N-a-t-u-s-k-a? Natuska. It might have been called Natuska, I'm not sure."

"And it's this book about it, written sometime after the 1930's, that you'd like to get a copy of?"

"Right. It must have been quite some time after, because those that had been there twenty or twenty-five years were called the pioneers."

"Well, here come Mr. Redondo and Miss Effingham now. Let's see if by any chance the book you want might be on the bookmobile."

Miss Dothan greeted the bookmobile librarian and the driver, and as they unlocked the bookmobile, she described the book which Mr. Tulare was seeking. Neither recalled seeing such a book among the stock on the bookmobile, nor did Miss Effingham, who had been bookmobile librarian for five years, even remember such a book. Miss Dothan returned to Mr. Tulare, who had been waiting outside the bookmobile door:

"Mr. Tulare, I don't think the book you want is on the bookmobile, but I'm going to try to locate it for you myself when I get back to the library and send it out to you. It may take a few days, because we'll have to identify the book first and then try to get it for you on interlibrary loan, if we don't have it ourselves. And if you'd like to see the Congressional documents about that investigation you mentioned, we might be able to get copies of those for you too."

"I'd like that, or anything you can find about it. But you mustn't put yourself to all that trouble."

"Oh, interlibrary loan is no trouble, once we know what we're looking for. And the same is true of government documents. We have all the indexes, and we usually can get what we want from one of the larger libraries in the state that is a depository for government publications."

"Is there a charge on that?"

"The costs are quite small, actually, and in this case the library is so indebted to you for taking care of the bookmobile all these years that this will be a way of showing our appreciation. You know, I might be able to find some books on that part of Alaska as it is today. Would you like to see those?"

"I surely would, or anything at all you might have on it."

The Maritza Public Library, which Miss Dothan directs, is located in a city of 43,000 people in the center of a sparsely settled region that is largely semi-rural and rural in character. The library serves an additional 10,000 or more county residents who live in unincorporated areas outside the city limits of Maritza. Of the staff of twenty, only Miss Dothan and the supervisor of children's services are library school graduates, although seven other members of the staff are classified as professionals by virtue of long experience and on the job training.

The Maritza Public Library has a collection of 110,000 volumes, approximately one third of which are juvenile titles. The reference collection numbers about 2,000 volumes and includes, as Miss Dothan's remarks to Mr. Tulare suggest, a complete run of the *Monthly Catalog of United States Government Publications* as well as the *Catalog of the Public Documents* which preceded it. Other major bibliographic reference works available include the *Cumulative Book Index* and *United States Catalog*, a full set of *Book Review Digest*, the complete "Standard Catalog" series, Public Affairs Information Service *Bulletin*, extensive runs of several Wilson periodical indexes, and the *Vertical File Index*. There is a twenty-year back file of the *New York Times Index*. The library owns the latest edition of the *Union List of Serials*, but does not subscribe to *New Serial Titles*, nor does the reference collection include any volumes of the printed catalogs of the Library of Congress or the *National Union Catalog*. In the atlas case are found *The Times Atlas* with its index, as well as several smaller American atlases. The library owns relatively recent printings of all the major American encyclopedias, as well as the usual quick-reference tools one would expect to find in a collection of this size which is kept reasonably up to date.

A limited book budget permits the library to purchase approximately 2,500 new adult titles each year, exclusive of duplicate copies. Subscriptions are maintained to about 200 current periodicals, including some gifts, which are retained in unbound back files for a maximum of ten years, because of space restrictions. The only exception to this policy is the bound file of the *National Geographic Magazine*, which is complete.

As the largest public library in the region, the Maritza Public Library draws directly on the state library for most interlibrary loans. Federal documents may be obtained on interlibrary loan either in microform or photocopy from the state university library, which is a partial depository, but which, because of limited staff, will not conduct searches from a subject point of view. Periodical articles may be obtained from the same source, under a similar restriction—that is, exact citations must be provided by the requesting library.

• • • • •

Who is the author and what are the title, publisher and date of publication of the book for which Miss Dothan is searching on behalf of Mr. Tulare? If this book is not in the collection of the Maritza Public Library, and cannot be borrowed from the state library, where can a copy be located? What are the Congressional documents that relate to the area of Alaska in which Mr. Tulare is interested? What other older or current materials relating to the subject can be located through sources that are known to be available, or that might reasonably be assumed to be available, in the Maritza Public Library?

How would you evaluate Miss Dothan's handling of the "reference interview" with Mr. Tulare? Will additional information be needed from him in order to locate the book he has described, or an adequate substitute for it? Of the published material about the region in which Mr. Tulare is interested, which items would you make a special effort to get for him? Does it appear to you that any potential sources of information or material may be being overlooked by Miss Dothan?

28.
Performance Budgeting

· · · · · · · · · · · · · · · · · ·

When Charles Slidell, Associate Director for Readers Services of the Sarda University Library, arrived at the office of the Director of Libraries, James Cheverly, he found that Dr. Cheverly and Florence Ludlow, Associate Director for Technical Services, were already waiting for him. Dr. Cheverly casually waved him to a seat, and began:

"I don't want to delay either of you unduly, but I am glad you were able to come to the office for a few minutes this afternoon. To be as brief as possible, I wanted to let you both in on something I picked up by accident over at the Treasurer's Office this morning. It looks as if our new president is planning to announce some changes in budgeting procedure for next year. Rumor has it that we'll be shifting over to what's variously referred to as 'performance budgeting' or 'program budgeting' in place of the traditional line budget and the traditional budget categories for salaries, books, periodicals, and so forth that we've been using. Evidently, President Decorah will announce this change early next month, but fortunately I picked it up via the grapevine this morning, which gives us a little bit of a headstart.

"Personally, as I think you both know, I have had no experience with performance budgeting at all, and I know next to nothing about it. I think all three of us are probably in the same boat as far as that's concerned, aren't we?"

Both Mr. Slidell and Miss Ludlow nodded in agreement. Dr. Cheverly continued:

"I thought as much, and that's why I wanted to catch both of you today. I think the first order of business is to inform ourselves as quickly as possible about performance budgeting and how it is applied to academic libraries. Charlie, could you, or somebody in the reference department, do a quick literature search and pick out a few key books, or preferably articles, that we could use to brief ourselves on performance budgeting in libraries? I imagine the literature is huge, so you'll have to be quite selective. Could we do that before the end of the week, and have copies made for the three of us?"

"Sure, Jim. We'll get right on it."

"Good. Now, the other thing I want to suggest is that we three get to work as soon as we have the relevant background and decide on two things. First, is it possible for us to construct a meaningful operating budget for the coming year, next month, using performance budgeting? Is this a system that is applicable to academic library operations? I seem to recall that some libraries have had real problems in trying to use it, but my memory may be faulty on this. If we really think we can't adapt to performance budgeting, then I'd like to bring this to the president's attention before he announces any new budgeting procedure. Obviously, I wouldn't want to do this unless we can come up with pretty convincing evidence that performance budgeting is just not applicable to an academic library situation. Florence, did you want to say something at this point?"

"Well, I've had no more experience with performance budgeting than either of you, but I believe a number of colleges and universities are using it, so I presume their libraries must be using it too. I don't know very much about what problems they have with it, but I think it demands considerable quantification of activities and services. That might be quite a problem in Charlie's areas of service, like reference, for example. It wouldn't be difficult in technical services, but I'm not sure how you do it in reference."

Dr. Cheverly replied: "I think you may be right on both points, Florence. If other academic libraries are using performance budgeting, it's going to be difficult to convince our boy that we can't do it at Sarda. But if, after investigation, we feel it just would not be a meaningful or appropriate method of budget-making for us, I'm perfectly willing to try to talk Decorah out of it. I think you're also right in guessing that it may be particularly difficult to present the reference function in the context of a program budget. It may, for example, require records or kinds of data that we simply don't have. This is something Charlie, in particular, will need to give careful thought to before we get together again on this. We may need to ask for a delay of a year, or something like that, in order to develop whatever records are needed as a base for a program budget request. Again, we simply don't know, at this point, and that's why I'm suggesting we inform ourselves about performance budgeting as quickly as we can, identify the problems that may arise in trying to apply it here, and come to some decision about whether we can live with it."

The meeting concluded with Mr. Slidell's agreeing to bring together a few key readings on performance budgeting in academic libraries for his two colleagues and himself, and to determine what problems, if any, might be involved in applying the performance budgeting technique to the reference and circulation departments of the library, for which he was responsible. The group agreed to meet again in one week's time to consider further the anticipated change in budgeting procedure.

Sarda University is a privately supported institution with a current enrollment of 11,000 students, a majority of whom are undergraduates majoring in the liberal arts and sciences. At present, there are also about 1,200 candidates for masters and doctoral degrees in fourteen liberal arts disciplines.

In recent years, Sarda University, like most privately supported institutions of higher education, has found it impossible to balance income against steadily rising operating expenses. Sarda's newly appointed president was faced immediately with a huge deficit for the current year. Consequently, one of his first official acts was to declare a moratorium on hiring new personnel, including those who would normally have been engaged to fill vacancies caused by resignations or retirements, for all departments of the university. Within the past month, department heads have been advised by the president to reduce expenditures for the current academic year, and to anticipate even more serious budget cuts for the year following.

At Sarda University, all library operations are centralized. There are no branch or departmental libraries. The central library, with a collection of approximately 600,000 volumes, is organized along functional lines, with circulation, reference, acquisitions, cataloging and processing as the major departments. The professional staff numbers approximately thirty, with an equal number of supporting full time non-professional staff, plus nearly ninety part-time student assistants.

• • • • •

What readings would you recommend to the administrative officers of the Sarda University Library as background on the application of performance budgeting to academic libraries? What difficulties, if any, are likely to arise in applying performance budgeting to the reference department? What kinds of records will the reference department need to develop and maintain? What steps should be taken administratively by Mr. Slidell in anticipation of the establishment of this new budgeting procedure?

Considering the experience of other academic libraries and the special circumstances at Sarda University, should Mr. Slidell recommend to Dr. Cheverly that the library try to prevent the adoption of performance budgeting, or ask to be exempted from it either temporarily or permanently?

29.
Tracing an Ancestor

. . . .

Among the mail delivered to the desk of the head of the reference department at Medway University one morning was the following letter which carried a handwritten note from the director of libraries, to whom it was addressed, reading "route to reference department for reply":

Dear Sir or Madame:

My wife and I, now retired, have been planning for many years to tour the great battlefields of the Civil War, in which I have always been very interested because my ancestors served in the Union forces. My great uncle, John Joseph Crosby, U.S.M.C., was among them.

We are planning carefully because we want to see all the places connected with my family in the war between the states. I have done research in many fine libraries to establish facts and map out our trip. Now, I am forced to admit defeat on one point, which is why I hope your wonderful library can help me out. If anyone possesses this information, it must be you, because even the U.S. Government hasn't been able to help me.

We have a book, which was in the possession of my great uncle at the time he was discharged from military service in November, 1865, inscribed in this fashion:

John Joseph Crosby, U.S.M.C.
his book
wrote June 21, 1865
in the light house in Bay Point
where I am stationed

My question for your library is this. Where is Bay Point? Since he was discharged from the Marines at Brooklyn, N.Y., I am prepared to find out that it might even be in that neighborhood, but we are not familiar with the East, never having visited it.

This is a mystery the whole family would like to see solved. I hope with your wonderful library somebody there can give us the answer.

Yours truly,
Rudolph J. J. Crosby

The letter bore a return address which indicated that the writer lived several hundred miles from Medway University.

The Medway University Library is one of the largest and finest research libraries in the United States, with a collection of nearly three million volumes. The general reference collection contains a majority of the titles in Winchell's *Guide to Reference Books,* with the exception of those in less familiar non-European languages and those in such fields as agriculture, medicine, law, music and physical science, which are housed in separate departmental libraries. The library is well staffed and exceptionally well supported.

There is no stated policy with respect to providing reference service to those not connected with the university, although it is generally understood that the primary obligation of the library and its staff is to serve the instructional and research needs of the students and faculty of Medway University. Accordingly, the reference staff will not normally conduct extensive searches or undertake extended research on behalf of those who are not members of the university community, except in the case of distinguished scholars who are faculty members at other institutions. Similarly, although the reference resources of the library are available to anyone wishing to use them in person, borrowing privileges are restricted to Medway students and faculty. All researchers are expected to bear the cost of any duplication of materials which is necessary to their investigations. The reference department receives a dozen or so requests for assistance by letter each week, as well as many times that number of telephone inquiries, from individuals having no connection with the university.

•   •   •   •   •

If, as a member of the staff of the reference department of the Medway University Library, you were assigned to reply to Mr. Crosby's letter, how would you respond to it? Where is Bay Point? What information is available in print that is relevant to Mr. Crosby's inquiry? In what form would it be most appropriate to make this available to him? Is there any problem involved in handling this request by mail?

Would you consider it advisable for the Medway University Library to adopt a more specific policy with respect to providing reference service to those who have no direct connection with the university?

30.
Finding Out about Cities

· · · · · · · · · · · · · · · · · · · ·

The Chindwin Public Library is located in a suburban community of about 25,000 people, near a major coastal city. Twenty years ago, Chindwin was primarily known as a summer resort, with a winter population of under 8,000. New highway construction, however, has led to an increase in the year-round population, and has severely taxed all existing municipal facilities, particularly the public school system, which has been forced to go onto double sessions and to engage in a major school building program.

The Chindwin Public Library has also felt the need to expand its resources and staff in order to serve a larger population, but library needs have ranked low on the list of municipal priorities up to this point. School libraries were non-existent in Chindwin ten years ago, and even now they have barely developed beyond the rudimentary stage. Consequently, the public library carries the main burden of providing materials to children in support of the educational program of the public schools. This responsibility has occasioned great strain on the library's limited human and material resources.

Although the operating budget of the Chindwin Public Library has more than doubled in the last ten years, this has not been sufficient to keep pace with the growing demands for materials and services of an increasing population, particularly in light of the fact that nearly forty percent of the current budget for books and periodicals is used to purchase materials for children or titles related to school reading lists. The book collection, exclusive of the contents of the children's room, comprises about 35,000 volumes, perhaps a third of which should be discarded as out of date or little used. About 1,200 volumes were purchased for the collection during the past year. The library subscribes to eighty-five current periodicals. The reference collection is small and could correctly be described as slightly below average in quality for a library serving a community this size. A partial list of the contents of the reference collection will be found in the Appendix to this case study.

The staff of the Chindwin Public Library includes, in addition to the library director, two trained librarians. Mrs. Carthage is in charge of the children's room, which serves pre-school through grade eight, and Miss Brainerd is reference librarian for young adult and adult services. Both are customarily on duty five afternoons a week, Monday through Friday. The reference room, where Miss Brainerd has her desk, is connected by an intercom telephone with the children's room which is on another level of the library building.

One afternoon, Miss Brainerd was in the midst of trying to locate an analysis of W. H. Auden's poem "September 1, 1939" for a high school student (who had come to the library just before the assignment was due only to discover that every available book about Auden had been charged out by his classmates) when she saw Mrs. Carthage enter the reference room, followed by four children of elementary school age. Suggesting that the student check the *Essay and General Literature Index* for an analysis of the Auden poem, Miss Brainerd went over to where Mrs. Carthage stood waiting.

"Peggy, these children are fifth graders and they've been given an assignment that will require them to use the reference room, because I just don't have the sources they'll need downstairs. I thought I'd better come up with them and show you the assignment. I'm sure there'll be fifteen or twenty more this afternoon and tomorrow and I thought we ought to talk about how you want to handle it."

Mrs. Carthage produced a mimeographed sheet headed FINDING OUT ABOUT CITIES which read as follows:

The library is a good place to find information about places. Learn how to use the reference books in the library by finding the answers to these questions about your city:

1. How many people live in this city? (Get the most up-to-date information you can!) Do more people live there now than lived there ten years ago?
2. Which county is the city located in?

3. What other large cities are located within 300 miles of it?
4. What are its major industries?
5. What railroads, airlines and bus lines operate in it?
6. What is its elevation above sea level?
7. What percent of the population is over 65?
8. What percent is under 21?
9. Does it have hard or soft water?
10. Who is the mayor or chief elected official? Find out a few facts about him.

The library is a good place to find information about many things. The librarians will help you learn to use the reference books.

At the bottom of the mimeographed sheet was a final line reading "The name of your city is _____." On the sheet which Mrs. Carthage showed Miss Brainerd, the name "Atlanta, Georgia" had been added in pen on the blank line. Miss Brainerd handed the sheet back to the children's librarian with a puzzled look, and said:

"Marjorie, does each child have a different city?"

"Evidently. These other three have Houston, Denver, and San Antonio, so I presume every child has been given a different city."

"I gather you had no advance warning of this assignment?"

"None, but that's par for the course. The children have been given today and tomorrow to get the information."

"Who's the teacher?"

"A Miss Dalton. I don't know her."

"Have you talked with her about this?"

"No. I just learned about it fifteen minutes ago when these children appeared with the mimeographed sheets. I'll try to phone her if you want, though I don't know what good it will do. We'll have to handle it and help the children as best we can. Or rather you'll have to, because I know I haven't got the material they'll need in the children's room. You know about all I have are the children's encyclopedias, and they're none too recent."

"I know. I guess you'll have to let them come up here, though I don't know where I'll put them. I don't have seats for these four, let alone any others."

"Well, perhaps you want to pick out what I'd need from the reference collection and put it on a book truck downstairs for the next couple of days, until the assignment is over. What do you think? How should we handle it?"

· · · · ·

If you were in Miss Brainerd's place, how would you respond to Mrs. Carthage's final question? What sources, from among those that are known to be available (see Appendix), or might reasonably be expected to be available at the Chindwin Public Library, will be needed to provide the information about individual American cities called for in Miss Dalton's assignment? Can all the questions be answered with the resources available in the Chindwin Library?

Assuming that the children have been given no prior instruction in the use of the library, would you, if you were Miss Brainerd, attempt to provide it in the context of this assignment? Or would you simply assemble the relevant reference sources in one place and direct the children to them? Or handle the assignment in some other way?

As a practical matter, what can be done to guard against the library staff's being taken by surprise by assignments of this kind? How would you evaluate "Finding Out about Cities" as a library assignment?

APPENDIX

This is a partial list of the reference books in the Chindwin Public Library.

> *American Oxford Atlas*
> *Ayer and Son's Directory of Newspapers and Periodicals* (three years
>   old)
> *Biography Index* (complete)
> *Book of the States* (latest edition)
> *Britannica Book of the Year* (1938 to date)
> *Collier's Encyclopedia* (two years old)
> *Columbia Encyclopedia*
> *Columbia-Lippincott Gazetteer of the World*

County and City Data Book
Cowles Comprehensive Encyclopedia
Current Biography (partial set)
Economic Almanac (three years old)
Encyclopaedia Britannica (five years old)
Encyclopedia Americana (three years old)
Encyclopedia International (four years old)
Facts on File
Goode's World Atlas
Hammond Ambassador World Atlas
Historical Statistics of the United States
Information Please Almanac (current edition)
International Who's Who
Lincoln Library of Essential Information
Municipal Yearbook (current edition)
National Geographic Atlas of the World
National Geographic Magazine Cumulative Index
New Century Cyclopedia of Names
Political Handbook and Atlas of the World (current edition)
Public Affairs Information Service Bulletin (complete)
Rand McNally New Cosmopolitan World Atlas
Rand McNally Road Atlas
Shepherd's Historical Atlas
Statesman's Yearbook (four years old)
Statistical Abstract of the United States (current edition)
Times Atlas of the World
Vertical File Index
Webster's Biographical Dictionary
Webster's Geographical Dictionary
Who's Who in America
Who's Who of American Women
World Almanac (current edition)
World Book Atlas
World Book Encyclopedia (current edition)

31.
Scientific Information

· · · · · · · · · · · · · · · · ·

Among the morning mail placed on the desk of Margaret Kennet, reference librarian at Struma State University, was the following letter, printed in a large, childish hand on a sheet of lined notebook paper:

Dear librarian:

What I have is a simple problem but I have been unable to answer it with the material they have at this school.

I have become very much involved in the field of chick embryology and am interested in finding scientific information in books or magazines on the development of and caring for chicks in a germ-free environment. Would you please try to help me find some books or someone I can write to for information on this subject?

Thank you very much.

Yours truly,
Roger Neosho

The letter carried the return address of a state training school for delinquent boys located about one hundred miles from the Struma campus in the rural section of the state.

Struma State University has a current enrollment of 9,000 students, chiefly undergraduate, who pursue programs of study in its colleges of liberal arts, agriculture, engineering and education. The university library has a collection of approximately 250,000 volumes and maintains current subscriptions to over 600 periodicals and serial publications. The library is a selective depository for United States government publications. Current holdings of government documents, a majority of which are uncataloged, number approximately 75,000 items. The reference collection is of average size and quality for an institution of this size, numbering about 1,200 titles, including current bibliographies and serial indexes.

As a publicly supported institution, it is the policy of the Struma State University Library to lend books and provide reference service within the limits of available staff and materials, to residents of the state who lack adequate local public library service. After reading Roger Neosho's letter, Miss Kennet first checked several library directories to confirm her suspicion that the state training school from which he had written had neither a library nor a resident librarian. Next, she telephoned the College of Agriculture, but was unable to locate any faculty member familiar with current work relating to the raising of chicks in a bacterially free environment.

• • • • •

Given the sources which could be assumed to be available in the Struma State University Library, how would you go about locating information in response to Roger Neosho's question? What material is available in print on this aspect of chick embryology which would be suitable to send to him? What restrictions might be made on interlibrary loan or photocopying in this particular situation? What additional information, if any, would be needed before an appropriate selection of material could be made? Would it be appropriate, or possible, to send the names of individuals working in the field in which he is interested? Who are these individuals and where can they be contacted? Approximately how much time would be required to construct an adequate response to this mail inquiry?

32.
A Political Campaign

· · · · · · · · · · · · · · · · · ·

When George Hays, Assistant Director for Public Services of the Lachlan Public Library, arrived at his desk one day, he found an envelope marked "confidential" awaiting his attention. It contained a note from Elizabeth Berea, the director of the library and Mr. Hays' immediate supervisor, which read as follows:

> George:
>   I had a call at home last night from a Mr. Salina on behalf of Frank Colby. Some group or individual opposed to Colby's re-election is circulating an anonymous handbill quoting *A Genealogy of the Goshen Family* by Herington, which is identified as being in our collection (I checked this morning, and we do have it). The genealogy includes an entry on p. 179 for Cynthia Goshen, with a note that "her first marriage to Frank C. Colby of Lachlan was ended by a divorce." (I've marked the page of the Herington book and left it on your desk.) Ethel tells me we've had twenty-three requests for photocopies of that particular page in the last week.
>   According to Mr. Salina, the opposition is using this to discredit Colby with Catholic voters. The handbill is being mailed out in precincts where there's a heavy concentration of Catholics. Mr. Salina says Herington is incorrect, that Colby has been married only once (to his present wife), and that he's never even met any Cynthia Goshen. Colby became aware of the existence of the *Goshen Genealogy* over a year ago, and has tried to have the error corrected, but the compiler is dead and so the text stands as is. Of course Colby's opponent dis-

claims any knowledge either of the genealogy or of the handbills that are being mailed.

Mr. Colby's position, according to Mr. Salina, is that since we, along with the State Library, are identified on the handbill as owning the *Goshen Genealogy*, this gives a kind of official support to the attempt to defame Colby's reputation. Salina says the State Library has been informed of the situation and has agreed to withdraw the *Goshen Genealogy* from their shelves. Colby is requesting the same of us, on grounds that the genealogy is inaccurate and its availability here is injurious to his prospects for re-election. Colby will not make the request in writing, for obvious reasons. He would like a letter from us stating that the *Goshen Genealogy* has been withdrawn as inaccurate, to use if the thing becomes a public issue later in the campaign. Salina makes a very persuasive case for our doing this on grounds of "fair play." His position is that Colby is being defamed and has no way to correct Herington's mistake. When I hesitated, Salina told me "confidentially" that Colby intends to sue the Herington estate for libel as soon as the election is over, and that "it is Mr. Colby's view that the Lachlan Public Library and its principal officers can be held legally accountable for disseminating information which they now know to be both inaccurate and injurious to Mr. Colby's reputation." Salina says that public officials are not immune from tort action for libel.

I explained you are responsible for the reference and genealogy collection, and I said I'd have to consult with you. Salina wasn't happy with the delay, but will phone me tonight for our answer.

I'm off to Varda for the day, but would like to get together with you to discuss this when I get back at around four this afternoon.

Elizabeth

P.S. Didn't want to bother you about this late last night, and when I tried to reach you by phone early this a.m., Lil told me you'd already left for a meeting.

The Lachlan Public Library serves 275,000 people who live both in the city where it is located and in surrounding Ebro County. The library has been directed for the past ten years by Miss Berea, who is admired by all who know her as a capable, dedicated and effective administrator, with a special flair for community and public relations. The library enjoys strong financial support and has an excellent reputation both locally and throughout the state and region.

George Hays has been a member of the staff of the Lachlan Public Library for fourteen years. Three years ago, when Miss Berea drew up a new organization chart for the staff, Mr. Hays was given supervisory responsibility for all public service areas of the library, while retaining the duties of head of the Reference and Genealogy Department. Genealogy has long been an area of special interest for the reference department at Lachlan, and current holdings include more than four hundred separately published genealogical volumes.

Frank Colby is presently engaged in a bitter and closely contested campaign for election to a fourth term as Public Prosecutor of Ebro County, of which Lachlan is the county seat. He is considered an honest, dedicated, conscientious and responsible public official who enjoys the support of liberal and reform groups throughout the state. If re-elected county prosecutor, he is expected to be a strong candidate for a vacancy which will occur in two years' time upon the retirement of the state's senior Representative in the United States House. Colby is a Roman Catholic, as are slightly more than forty-five percent of the registered voters in Ebro County.

• • • • •

If you were in Mr. Hays' place, what recommendation would you make to Miss Berea concerning the request by Frank Colby's representative that Herington's *Genealogy of the Goshen Family* be suppressed and repudiated by the Lachlan Public Library? In a situation of this kind, can the library be held responsible in either a legal or a moral sense for the veracity of information contained in reference books on its shelves?

33.
A Research Assignment

. . . .

George Bedford, Associate Director for Reader's Services at Aldan University Library, had just finished looking through the morning mail when the telephone on his desk rang:

"Readers Services, Mr. Bedford."

"Mr. Bedford, Ralph Crowley here, editor of *Aldan Today*, the alumni magazine. Ed Mayfield suggested I call you."

"Yes, Mr. Crowley, what can I do for you?"

"I'm hoping you can give me some help on an article we're planning for the fall issue, some research help."

"Sure thing! Glad to help any way we can."

"Mr. Bedford, did you, by any chance, know Leon Prestonburg?"

"No, I'm sorry to say, I didn't, although, of course, I've heard of him. He was dean of men for thirty years or more at Aldan, wasn't he?"

"Thirty-four years, to be exact. He was something of an institution at Aldan. A grand old man. We had over 1,200 alumni turn out for his retirement party."

"He retired just before I came to Aldan. Is he still living?"

"Yes, he is. In fact, I talked with him on the telephone just this morning. I've persuaded him to do a piece for *Aldan Today*. That's why I called you, in hopes that the library could give him a hand with some background material. Leon really can't get out to do any research himself these days, but he said if the library could put together enough background material for him, he'd get the piece written."

"We'll be more than willing to try. What is the piece about?"

"Well, the idea is this. You know, academic administrators—college presidents, deans, and so on—have really been getting it in the neck lately with all the problems on college and university campuses. The press—even the alumni press—is just filled with tales of one college president after another who's made a mess out of a campus problem. The image of the academic administrator is pretty rotten these days."

"I agree, it sure is."

"Well, we thought somebody should present the other side. Do a piece featuring presidents and deans who've been successful, handled tough problems well, that sort of thing. For example, take the dean who deliberately hires a controversial faculty member, who sticks his neck out in the interest of academic freedom. That's the sort of thing we had in mind. I called Leon and he loved the idea. Sort of a *Profiles in Courage* type of piece is what he has in mind. However, the problem is that the old boy's been out of touch for nine years. He doesn't really know much about what's going on in university circles these days. Doesn't know the people. So what I thought was that the library could find the material for him. Could you?"

"We can try. You want examples of academic administrators who've been succesful in handling touchy or difficult problems, is that it?"

"Yes, examples of that and biographical information on the people involved, that Leon can use as background."

"I think I understand what you're after. I imagine you'd like several examples?"

"I'd think at least a half dozen current or recent ones. More if possible. It will be a short article, because we're hoping to place it in the newspapers as well as in *Aldan Today*. It's all quite tentative at this point, but I can tell you confidentially we've got a good shot at making the most influential daily in the state, if you people can come up with what Leon needs."

"As I said, we'll gladly try. How soon do you need it?"

"By the end of the week, if possible. I'm driving out to see Leon on Saturday, and I promised to bring whatever was available with me."

Aldan University boasts one of the larger academic research libraries in the United States. There are more than one and a half million volumes in the collection, with nearly 6,000 titles in general reference. The library accessioned over 15,000 items in the past year and maintains current subscriptions to more than 3,000 periodicals.

. . . . .

Assuming that you have been assigned the task of compiling background information for the alumni magazine article which former Dean Prestonburg plans to write, what sources would you use to locate the desired material and in what order would you consult them? Indicate specific items of information which you would plan to bring to the prospective author's attention. How much time do you estimate would be required to conduct the search and assemble the needed materials? What additional information, if any, might Mr. Bedford have obtained that would have facilitated the search?

34.
A Technical Institute
· · · · · · · · · · · · · · · ·

On the morning of his second day as Senior Consultant for Special Projects at the B___ State Library, George Lewes received a call from Irene Wilton, the Associate State Librarian, asking him to join her in her office as soon as possible. Mr. Lewes appeared in Mrs. Wilton's office about five minutes later, and was greeted warmly by his supervisor:

"George, I'm sorry to drag you up here but I'm scheduled to testify at a Ways and Means Committee hearing at 10:30 this morning and I did want to catch you before I left, both to be sure you were getting settled all right and to alert you to your first 'special project' which will be coming in to see you this afternoon."

"I'm getting settled just fine, Mrs. Wilton. Of course, it's all pretty new and confusing at this point, especially coming from a college library where the whole environment is completely different, but I'm sure I'll eventually catch on to who everybody is and what they're up to."

"You'll have a chance to start this afternoon. Fred Hamden, the President of Teviot Technical Institute, will be coming in to see you. Teviot is a two-year, publicly supported junior college upstate. Up until about five or six years ago, it was a kind of county agricultural school that was dying, because fewer and fewer young people are going in for careers in agriculture. Then Hamden was appointed president, and set about converting the school from agriculture to engineering technology. He's apparently been quite successful in getting both state and federal vocational education money for this changeover to engineering, though the school is still under control of a county board."

"I see. Where do I and the state library come in?"

"Teviot has no trained librarian. Hamden's been trying to hire one, without success, for over a year, or so he tells me. He's asking for help from us because he's got to spend a big chunk of money in a hurry. He wants to use it to buy reference books, because he wants to upgrade the library in anticipation of applying for accreditation."

"How much has he got to spend for books?"

"I think he said $35,000. And the money has to be spent by the end of this fiscal year, June 30."

"Wow! This is May 15."

"Right! That leaves about six weeks. That's one reason he's decided to buy reference books. They're expensive and he can get the money spent quickly that way. But he has no idea at all of what reference books to buy. He's had visits from a couple of salesmen—publishers' representatives —who want to sell him 'package libraries' of their own firm's publications, but I urged him against doing this. Instead, I've suggested that you draw up a buying list for him. Think you can do it?"

"I'll be glad to try, if that's the assignment. But I don't have any subject background in science or engineering at all, as I think you know."

"Neither has anybody else on the consultant staff, George. My first thought, I must admit, was to suggest to President Hamden that he hire a science literature or science reference specialist as a consultant. But, it turns out Teviot has no money for consultant services. That's how it always is in our business, you know; all the money in the world for books, but no money for staff to select them intelligently."

"But he must have had money budgeted for a librarian's salary for this year. If he hasn't been able to hire one, couldn't he get permission to use some of that for a consultant?"

"He tried and was turned down by the county board. And he does have a librarian, of sorts. Myrtle Logan, a very nice woman who used to be the town librarian in Teviot before she retired, now works half-time at the Institute."

"Is she a trained person?"

"No, Myrtle is just a high school graduate. She ran the public library in Teviot, a town of only about 1,000 people, for years and years. Very devoted, but quite old school and highly limited. I gather she minds the circulation desk at the Institute and has 'cataloged' in some way or another the few books they have, but she'll have nothing to do with book selection. Mr. Hamden knows her limitations, but she's the closest thing to a librarian he's been able to come up with. And we're the only consultant

service he has available to him, so we'll just have to do our best to help
him out. Or, rather, you'll have to do your best."

"Of course, Mrs. Wilton. There is one thing I'd like to ask you,
though. I'm new on this job, and I don't know yet what my other responsibilities will be, or how much time they will take. About how much
time should I put in on this Teviot project?"

"To a certain extent, George, you'll have to develop the ability to
gauge this sort of thing for yourself, and be responsible for your own time.
But, your question is a perfectly legitimate one at this point. I'd say, in
total, Teviot Technical Institute might be worth as much as a working week
of your time over the next month or so. This represents a real opportunity
for the agency for a couple of reasons. Teviot is a pet project of Senator
Blackstone, who's the ranking majority party member in the legislature
and a very important man when the time comes around for appropriations
for the state library. President Hamden and the Senator are great friends,
I gather. In fact, it was Blackstone who referred Mr. Hamden to us. But
beyond that, the state library has, very properly I think, been criticized for
neglecting colleges and universities and devoting our time to public and
school libraries. That's chiefly because the federal and state programs we
administer are concerned almost exclusively with public and school libraries,
and because most of us on the staff are public or school library people. So,
the Teviot project is a nice opportunity to show we're interested in academic libraries too."

"I see. You think about a week's time in all?"

"More or less. I'd get as full a briefing as you can from President
Hamden when he comes in this afternoon. Then, I'd imagine you'd want
to go up to Teviot for a day or so to see what the situation there is like,
talk to the faculty, and so on, so as to be able to make an intelligent selection of reference books for them. I assume there are standard lists available
that you can draw on to make up a buying list, but I think it's important
to tailor your selection to their specific needs as much as you can, within
the time limits you have to work under."

"O.K., Mrs. Wilton. I'll be looking for President Hamden this afternoon. It should be an interesting initial project for me."

"I'm sure you'll do a fine job. It's exactly the kind of thing we hired
you to do, and a perfect illustration of why I was eager to create the position of Consultant for Special Projects. If you remember, back when I first
talked with you about joining our staff, I stressed that we wanted a 'flexi-

ble' person, a person who could work intensively on a special assignment for a short period of time, clean it up, and move on to something quite different."

"Well, I'll try to get things off to a good start with the Teviot project."

Later that day, Mr. Lewes spent several hours with President Hamden, who proved to be a dynamic, outgoing man endowed with a magnetic personality and a clear vision of a glowing future for Teviot Technical Institute. Hamden told Lewes that Teviot was "almost at the point of extinction" when he became its president six years earlier. One year after President Hamden's arrival, Teviot Agricultural Institute became Teviot Technical Institute, and new curricula were established in electrical and mechanical engineering. Two years later, industrial and electronic engineering programs were added. In five years' time, enrollment had grown from fewer than 50 to 175 full-time students, and the size of the full-time faculty had increased from 4 to 18. President Hamden predicted that both the student body and the faculty would double in size within the next ten years, and that at least one new program of study, aviation engineering, would be added.

The library was currently housed in a new dormitory, although a separate library building was planned for the future. President Hamden said that the library was a matter of the gravest concern to him at present, as he was preparing to seek both regional and professional accreditation for the Institute during the coming year, and had already been advised that the library "did not measure up to standards." Although he had successfully obtained a grant of $35,000 in vocational education funds for books, with the proviso that the money be expended during the current year, his efforts to recruit a librarian had failed. "So, you see, Mr. Lewes," President Hamden concluded, "this is why I'm here, seeking your help. We must spend $35,000 on reference books within the next six weeks, and there is nobody to tell us what we need to buy. Can you do the job for us?"

"I'll certainly be glad to try, Mr. Hamden, and I think we can manage it. But what about the faculty? Have you asked them to recommend books?"

"Mr. Lewes, the thing I'm proudest of about our engineering faculty is that every one of them has come to the school direct from industry. These men are not the kind you'd find teaching in a college of engineering. There isn't a Ph.D. in the lot of them, and I wouldn't want one. We're training boys to work on the production line and in the drafting room—to do highly practical work. And the kind of man to teach them is a man who's come right out of the drafting room himself. They're superb teachers, and I can tell you that industry is clamoring for our boys because of the kind of teachers they have. But these men know very little about library books, Mr. Lewes. If you expect a lot of suggestions from them, I'm afraid you'll be disappointed."

Mr. Lewes' two-day visit to Teviot Technical Institute the following week confirmed all that President Hamden had told him in advance. He inspected the library and found it contained only about 2,000 volumes, at least half of which seemed to have little relevance either to the teaching program or to the current interests of students. Of the approximately 200 titles in the "reference collection," perhaps half could have been discarded with no great loss. He discovered that the library had current subscriptions to about sixty periodicals, a considerable number of which fell into the category of strictly recreational reading. There were no significant back files of periodicals. During his visit, Mr. Lewes held individual conferences with all full-time members of the faculty. He found that they were likeable men with impressive backgrounds in private industry and a strong collective commitment to teaching. He also found that a few of them had developed small reference libraries of books and pamphlets in their offices or class-rooms, but that a majority made little use of printed materials instruc-tionally, beyond basic textbooks which their students purchased. Nor, with one exception, did any of the faculty appear to understand or be more than politely interested in the several ways in which Mr. Lewes suggested the library might be made a more integral part of the teaching process. The single exception was the chairman of the faculty library committee, a young man who taught courses in writing and communication skills, and who had taken the trouble to familiarize himself with the ACRL *Standards for Junior College Libraries.* He indicated that he had tried repeatedly during the three years he had been at Teviot to interest other members of the faculty in recommending books for the library, but to no avail. Mr. Lewes dis-covered that most of the books purchased up to that point had been selected by this man, usually on the recommendations of textbook salesmen, who were referred to him whenever they visited the campus. He also discovered that this man would be leaving Teviot at the end of the current academic year.

Mr. Lewes found the curriculum at Teviot organized into three major segments. Each student devoted approximately twenty-five percent of his time to what was termed "general education," twenty-five percent to "basic sciences," and the balance to "engineering sciences." By way of illustration, a student pursuing the curriculum in electrical engineering technology would complete the following courses over a two-year period:

FIRST YEAR

First Semester	*Second Semester*
Communication skills	Communication skills
Technical math	Technical math
Physics	Electrical physics
Mechanical drawing	Electrical drafting
Fabrication processes	A.C. Circuits
D.C. Circuits	Instruments
Physical education	Physical education

SECOND YEAR

First Semester	*Second Semester*
Psychology	Logic
Calculus	Industrial psychology
Business economics and law	Technical report writing
Electrical machines and controls	Electrical construction
Power transmission	Problem analysis
A.C. Circuits	Electronics

Students in the other engineering specializations followed parallel curricula.

Before leaving Teviot, Mr. Lewes met briefly with President Hamden to discuss the results of his visit. He suggested that, for the purposes of developing a buying list for immediate purchase, the term "reference book" be defined quite broadly, to include not only titles for the non-circulating reference collection, but basic monographs and journal files both of a general nature and in the particular subject fields related to the Teviot engineering curricula. Hamden agreed, although he pointed out the desirability of using the present grant to order more costly items of permanent value, as well as titles which could be obtained quickly in order to encumber all available funds before the end of the fiscal year five weeks hence. Mr. Lewes agreed to include in his report recommendations of specific dealers from whom books could be purchased quickly, and cautioned against ordering books directly from publishers because this might result in long delays in filling orders. He was also asked by President Hamden to suggest procedures for the orderly development of the collections in the coming year, on the assumption that a professionally trained librarian could not be found to take responsibility for the Teviot Library.

• • • • •

Assuming that, like Mr. Lewes, you have no special subject background in engineering or science, how would you go about developing a buying list for Teviot Technical Institute in order to meet a deadline five weeks hence? Are there, as Mrs. Wilton suggested, standard lists available which might be used? Identify each of these, indicate specifically how it would be used in this project, and what its limitations would be. What portion of the available funds would you allocate for general reference works? What major general reference works would you recommend be purchased? What portion of available funds would you allocate for journal files? What specific titles should be purchased? In which subject areas would you recommend titles for purchase? How would you go about selecting these? What criteria and sources would you use? What recommendations would you make with respect to suppliers, and with respect to the problem of creating machinery for book selection during the coming year, assuming that the services of a qualified librarian cannot be obtained in the next twelve months? Your recommendations should take into account the fact that Mr. Lewes has no more than three working days at a maximum remaining to devote to the Teviot Technical Institute book selection project.

35.
Project SLAT

· · · · · · · · · · ·

During the months immediately preceding her graduation from library school, Marie Lubec investigated potential employment opportunities in more than two dozen academic libraries before accepting a position as reference assistant at Chenab University. She chose Chenab from among several job offers because the salary was attractive, the campus was located in a pleasant semi-rural town within an hour's drive of a large city, the library had an excellent reputation and, chiefly, because she had been so favorably impressed by the personality and professional attitude of the director, Edward Boone. During his recruiting trip to her school, and subsequently, when she spent two days visiting the Chenab campus while considering the job offer Boone had made to her, she sensed a genuine spirit of innovation and change in the library. Boone seemed to overflow with ideas and energy. He spoke frequently, during her visit to Chenab, about the necessity of "finding new ways to make the library more relevant to all phases of student life," of "breaking down outdated traditional staffing patterns," and of "making the library the focus of the instructional program." Mr. Boone seemed to Marie Lubec to have a genuine commitment to change and a receptivity to new ideas and new ways of doing things which she found highly refreshing by contrast with the attitudes of the administrators of most of the other academic libraries with which she was familiar. Immediately after returning from her visit to Chenab, she wrote Mr. Boone accepting the position he had offered her as one of three professional librarians in the reference department. He responded with a prompt and cordial letter confirming her appointment to the staff.

Several weeks later, during the period between the end of the spring semester and the beginning of the summer session, Miss Lubec received a further communication from Mr. Boone in the form of a note stapled to a longer memorandum:

Dear Miss Lubec:

I am just leaving for an extended vacation (my first in a good many years). I will be returning to the campus in early September, a few days after you will have officially joined us, and I will be looking forward to seeing you then. Meanwhile, I wanted to write you before leaving because we have decided to put you in charge of our new SLAT project starting in the fall.

During our conversations this spring, I think I mentioned that one of my great concerns at Chenab is to break out of traditional patterns of staffing reference service and find new ways to utilize non-professionals. Project SLAT is a first step in this direction. The enclosed press release will give you the basic format of SLAT, but beyond this the responsibility for defining the content of the training program and directing it will be yours. I wanted you to have some advance warning, and particularly, since our professional collection in library science is limited, to take advantage of your library school library this summer to investigate new approaches in training student assistants and non-professionals which might have been employed elsewhere and could be adapted to Project SLAT.

I hope you will be able to work out the plans for the new training program in some detail before you get here, because the project must get underway early in September. Since you will doubtless want to put in a good deal of time on the project this summer, I have made arrangements for your salary here to begin on August 1, even though you will not arrive on the campus until September 1. In this way, we can compensate you for your time this summer.

The five trainees have already been selected and notified to report to you in the library during freshman orientation week. I hope you will come up with a really innovative and meaningful training program, not just a watered down version of traditional library school courses. Best of luck with the assignment. I'll be eager to see the results in September.

> Cordially,
> Edward C. Boone, Director

Enclosed with Mr. Boone's letter was a press release, dated a few days earlier:

CHENAB LIBRARY AWARDED GRANT FOR PROJECT SLAT

Edward C. Boone, Director of the Chenab University Library, announced today that the library has been awarded a grant of $25,000 through the Chenab University Research Council for a pilot program to train student library assistants. Designated as Project SLAT (Student Library Assistant Training), the new program will provide for recruiting and training five incoming freshmen from low income families each year. After an initial training year, the participants will continue as regular part-time employees of the Chenab Library throughout their remaining three years at the university. Each student participant will receive five hours of formal instruction in library techniques and skills per week, and will devote an equal amount of time to supervised work in the library's reference department.

Boone termed Project SLAT a "breakthrough in finding new sources of trained manpower for academic libraries." "Chenab, like most college and university libraries, has always used student assistants," he said, "but only in the most routine, menial and uninteresting jobs." This is because academic libraries have not, up until now, recognized their responsibility to train students for more meaningful job assignments. "Project SLAT," according to Boone, "will make it possible for the Chenab University Library to develop and carry out an innovative training program comprising about 150 hours of formal instruction, tailored specifically to student assistants." He expects that those who complete the training program will be able to provide skilled bibliographic and reference assistance to students and faculty, especially during evening and weekend hours, when members of the regular library staff are not available to cover the reference desk. Boone pointed out that "for decades academic libraries have failed to utilize the full potential of student assistants, while at the same time students and members of the faculty have suffered from lack of trained staff." Project SLAT is designed to develop a corps of students to replace reference librarians during off-hours. Trainees will also learn to compile bibliographies, fill interlibrary loan requests and conduct searches on behalf of the library's acquisitions department.

Boone lauded the University Research Council for what he termed "a far-seeing decision which should result in better library service to the 9,000 students and more than 1,000 members of the faculty and staff of Chenab University." Grant funds will be used to pay salaries of the trainees and to purchase or develop training materials, as well as to pay a portion of the salary of the project director, who will devote one third of her time to Project SLAT during the coming year. Mr. Boone announced that Miss Marie Lubec, who will join the staff in September, upon completion of graduate study in library science at Dniester University, will direct the project. Boone said that Miss Lubec was selected as project director "because we wanted to have a young person who could work well with students, as well as one who is new to the staff and therefore not tied to existing patterns of operation, since the SLAT trainees will be expected to learn to perform many tasks that have traditionally been handled only by library school graduates." He emphasized that there are no existing models for the type of training program to be conducted at Chenab. Trainees have already been selected for the coming year by the University Student Financial Aid Office on the basis of need and family income.

• • • • •

Outline in as much detail as possible the training program which you would propose to conduct at Chenab University if you were director of Project SLAT. Indicate specific topics to be covered, the amount of time to be devoted to each, and the specific training methods to be employed. What training materials exist that could be considered for use in such a program? How would you evaluate these generally and in terms of the requirements of Project SLAT? What specific kinds of new training materials would need to be developed? What models exist for training programs for reference personnel at this level?

Do you feel the basic concept of Project SLAT is sound? What benefits might accrue to the university, the library, students and faculty if the project is successful? What limitations, if any, does the proposal seem to have? What specific tasks from the traditional list of professional and non-professional duties in academic library reference departments would you feel the Project SLAT trainees should be instructed in?

Selected Bibliography

· · · · · · · · · · · · · · · · ·

I. COLLECTIONS OF INSTRUCTIONAL CASE STUDIES IN LIBRARY SCIENCE

Coburn, Louis. *Case Studies in School Library Administration*. Flushing, N.Y.: Queens College, 1968.

Galvin, Thomas J. *Problems in Reference Service*. New York: Bowker, 1965.

Grogan, Denis. *Case Studies in Reference Work*. Hamden, Conn.: Archon Books, 1967.

Hewitt, Roy. *Library Management Case Studies*. London: Crosby Lockwood, 1969.

Kister, Kenneth F. *Social Issues and Library Problems*. New York: Bowker, 1968.

Lowell, Mildred H. *The Management of Libraries and Information Centers*. Metuchen, N.J.: Scarecrow Press, 1968. 3 vols.

Metcalf, Keyes D. *Studies in Library Administrative Problems*. New Brunswick, N.J.: Graduate School of Library Service, Rutgers, The State University, 1960.

Ranganathan, S. R. *Reference Service*. 2d ed. New York: Asia Publishing House, 1961.

Shaffer, Kenneth R. *The Book Collection*. Hamden, Conn.: Shoe String Press, 1961.

———. *Library Personnel Administration and Supervision*. 3d ed. Hamden, Conn.: Shoe String Press, 1968.

———. *Twenty-five Cases in Executive-Trustee Relationships in Public Libraries*. Hamden, Conn.: Shoe String Press, 1960.

Slavens, Thomas P., ed. *Library Case Studies in the Social Sciences*. Ann Arbor, Mich.: Campus Publishers, 1967.

II. THE CASE METHOD OF TEACHING

Andrews, Kenneth R., ed. *The Case Method of Teaching Human Relations and Administration*. Cambridge: Harvard University Press, 1960.

Copeland, Melvin T. *And Mark an Era: The Story of the Harvard Business School.* Boston: Little Brown, 1958.

Galvin, Thomas J. "A Case Method Approach in Library Education," *Library School Teaching Methods: Courses in The Selection of Adult Materials.* Edited by Larry Earl Bone. Urbana, Ill.: University of Illinois, Graduate School of Library Science, 1969. pp. 60–72.

————. "Case Studies and Case Method." *Encyclopedia of Library and Information Science.* vol. IV.

Hewitt, Roy. "Case Studies and Their Place in Education for Librarianship," *The Library World,* LXIX (July 1967), 8–10.

McNair, Malcolm P., ed. *The Case Method at the Harvard Business School.* New York: McGraw Hill, 1954.

Needham, Christopher D. "Particulars and Principles: Case Studies in Librarianship," *Journal of Librarianship,* II (Jan. 1970), 56–71.

Pigors, Paul and Pigors, Faith. *Case Method in Human Relations: The Incident Process.* New York: McGraw Hill, 1961.

"A Reference Encounter." *Library Journal,* April 15, 1965, 1818–1824.

Schnelle, Kenneth E. *Case Analysis and Business Problem Solving.* New York: McGraw Hill, 1967.

Shaffer, Kenneth R. "The Case Method in Library Education," *College and Research Libraries,* XIX (Nov. 1958), 487–490.

————. "Personnel Administration: The Case Method of Teaching," *Bulletin of the Medical Library Association,* LIII (Oct. 1965), 546–551.

Sherwood, Frank P. and Storm, William B., eds. *Teaching and Research in Public Administration: Essays on the Case Approach.* Los Angeles: School of Public Administration, University of Southern California, 1960.

Stenzel, Anne K. and Feeney, Helen M. *Learning by the Case Method: Practical Approaches for Community Leaders.* New York: Seabury Press, 1970.